BEGINNING BACKGAMMON

Also available from The Lyons Press

100 Backgammon Puzzles

Beginning Chess

The Right Way to Play Chess

BEGINNING BACKGAMMON

STRATEGY AND TACTICS FOR WINNING PLAY

J. DU C. VERE MOLYNEUX

THE LYONS PRESS
Guilford, Connecticut
An imprint of The Globe Pequot Press

CONTENTS

1

INTRODUCTION

What is backgammon?

TABLES – the family of games to which backgammon belongs – is one of the oldest surviving, second in this respect only to mancala. A form of tables was played in ancient Egypt, some four thousand years ago. It spread to Athens and from there to the Roman Empire. The Romans enlarged the board, increased the number of points and men, and made it 'a game in a box', similar to the backgammon of today.

It is not certain what sort of games were played on the tables in the past, but we can assume that the men's moves were regulated by dice rolls, and single pieces – "blots" – were vulnerable. In some games they seemed to use three dice.

When the two dice were introduced, or when the game now known as backgammon was invented, is open to speculation. It is certain, though, that in the middle ages backgammon was so popular that all attempts by the political and clerical authorities to have it banned were failures.

No game survives for thousands of years by chance. The reasons for backgammon's lasting popularity are too complex to list – let alone analyse – in a short introductory note. But we should mention in brief the basic ingredients of its perennial appeal.

First and foremost, backgammon is a delightfully challenging game. Its simplicity of form conceals a perfect inner mechanism. The rules are all in perfect harmony with the game's objectives.

Secondly, it attracts players of contrasting mentalities and motivations, for it can be at one time a vicious gambling game, and on a different occasion a pleasant family pastime. Unlike poker, backgammon may be played for no stakes at all – and yet be thoroughly enjoyed. Moreover, an average standard of competence is a social asset since the game is so universally popular.

Finally, its combination of skill and luck enables players of differing skill and aptitude to play together for long periods without boredom or one-sided results.

This book has been written with the complete beginner in mind. I have assumed that the reader has no knowledge of backgammon and so I use simple language and plenty of diagrams to describe how the game is played.

The first six chapters deal with the necessary equipment, the initial set up, the best opening moves – also giving alternatives, where necessary – the basic types of game, the elementary tactics and the overall strategy. They also refer to the dice probabilities and the gambling aspects – including the right use of the doubling cube. A sample game shows how the theories are transformed into practice. There are plenty of illustrations and a roll-to-roll analysis – so the reader does not actually need to study the book with a backgammon board at his side.

The last chapters describe the best alternative games of the tables' board, with rules, illustrations and hints on play. Some of these may come as a pleasant surprise, if not a revelation, to the reader.

The final chapter evaluates some possible experiments on the backgammon board. It examines, for instance, the possibility of using dominoes instead of dice, and how the traditional game may be affected by this. It also describes, in some detail, one diceless game, "Grasshopper", which is played like a game of chess.

Throughout the book, I have endeavoured to describe the rules clearly and to explain to the reader their logical or common-sense necessity. My sole advice to the beginner is to avoid skipping chapters out of impatience, and to check the rules with the diagrams that illustrate them. From this point of view, this book is complete in itself.

2

EQUIPMENT AND RULES

Equipment

TO PLAY backgammon, you need a backgammon board. There are plenty available at different prices, but it is advisable to choose a solidly-made wooden set, with reasonably large men that can be handled easily. Backgammon is not a game limited to any particular age group, so your set should be solid enough to serve you for a lifetime – and to stand some unavoidable abuse.

Wooden boards come in various sizes. Some are lined, some unlined; this makes no difference. A medium-sized board, ten to thirteen inches long, is generally the most convenient. A first-time buyer should also check the pieces ("men"). They should not be rough or chipped, and their colours should be "pure", that is without any tiny spots or blemishes. A complete backgammon set consists of:

A board in the form of a box.
Thirty men in two contrasting colours – fifteen in each colour.
Two pairs of dice.
Two dice cups ("shakers").
One doubling cube.

Should your opponent ask to use the same pair of dice as you, there is no reason to refuse. Or he may reasonably ask for the dice to be mixed up. Even if you do not gamble, nothing could more spoil the pleasure of a game than any suspicion of biased equipment. For the same reason, you should insist on the use of dice cups, to guarantee a clean and fair throw. Rolling the dice from the hand is not satisfactory. These may seem small points, but the proper "etiquette" is essential for the enjoyment of any game, especially one depending on dice.

Board, men and notation

The box is divided into two pairs of *tables* by a partition known as the *bar*. The two tables in front of you are your outer and inner tables. Each table consists of six *points*. The points are arranged in alternate colours or shades, usually dark and light. This is to facilitate counting when the players move their men from one point to another.

Having chosen the colour of your men, you proceed to decide which one of the two tables in front of you will be your *inner table* (the other becomes automatically your *outer table*). There is no strict rule to stipulate which is your inner table. In the pre-electricity era, when candles or lamps were the sole means of lighting, the rule was that "the inner table must be closer to the light". Even today, some daylight players choose the window as the reference point to locate their inner tables.

In this book we shall adopt a number of conventions which will enable the reader to identify the position and the moves of his men and thus learn the rules more easily.

First, no matter what the actual colour of the men in your set is, for the purposes of this book they are called *black* and *white*. The player who has chosen the black men is called the *black player*, and the one who plays with the white men is the *white player*.

Second, in the diagrams we shall place the black player at the top of the board and the white player at the bottom.

So far as notation is concerned, there are many systems

but no single one seems to be universally accepted. The least confusing system is to number the 24 points of the board from 1 to 12 twice over – once for the white and once for the black.

Points 1 to 6 are the inner tables; 7 to 12 the outer tables. They face each other. Diagram 1 shows this arrangement.

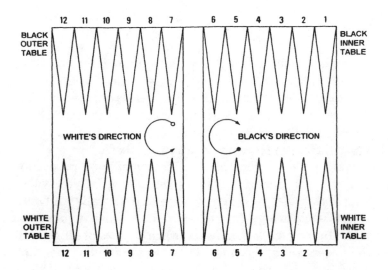

1.   Board and notation system.

Set-up and dice rolls

At the outset the two players arrange their men as in Diagram 2. Note that five men are already in their respective inner tables. Three men in their outer tables. Five men in the opponent's outer table. And two men ("the runners") in the opponent's inner table. White moves in an anticlockwise direction, black moves clockwise. See Diagram 2.

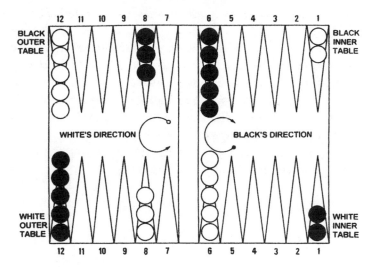

2.   The initial set-up.

Object

To bring all your men into your inner table and then bear them off (take them off the board). Winner is the player who first bears off all his men. A tie is not possible.

First player

To decide who plays first, both players throw *one* die. (If both are the same, the result is ignored and both throw again – a game cannot start with a double.) The higher number wins and, in most schools, plays the combined numbers of both throws, although in many continental European countries the first player has the option to reject the combined throw and throw again. If a match is played, the winner of the previous game plays first in the next one, unless otherwise agreed.

Dice

To move or bear off your men you have to use your dice. Each player, in his turn, places his two dice in his dice cup, shakes them (hence these cups are also called "shakers") and throws them in his *right-hand* half of the board. If a die jumps off or does not fall flat, the throw must be re-taken. The numbers on the tops of the dice are called the dice roll and regulate how many points you may move your men. For instance, a roll of 5-3 stipulates that either

— you have to move one man five points and another three, or

— you have to move one man eight points, being the total of the two dice, provided that his way is not blocked, as explained later (see *Moving*). Diagram 3 shows two ways of moving to a throw of 5-3.

If you roll a double (sometimes known as a "doublet",

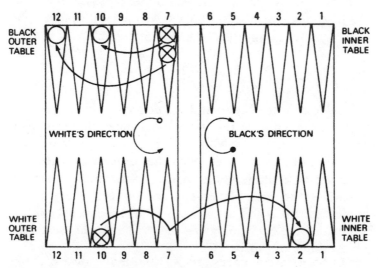

3. Two ways to play 5–3.

two 3s for instance) you must move your men twice as many times. Thus you may move

— *One man*: twelve points.
— *Two men*: six points each, or one man nine points and one man three points.
— *Three men*: two of them three points each, and the third six points.
— *Four men*: three points each.

It is assumed that the moves are permissible within the rules of moving (below). Diagram 4 shows four different ways of moving to a throw of double three (3-3).

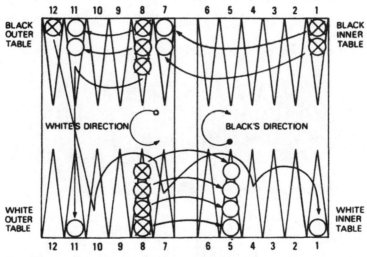

4. Four ways to play 3–3.

Moving

Men never move backwards. They move towards their destinations, which are their respective inner tables.

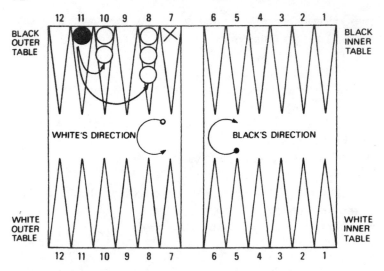

5. 3–1. Black is unable to move.

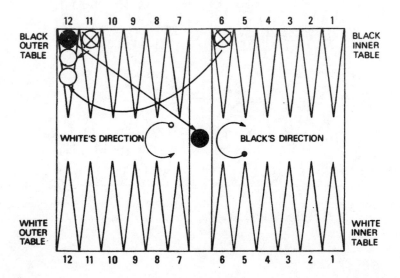

6. 6–1. Two white men hit a blot, which is placed on the bar.

Moves are taken individually. Strictly speaking, 3-1 does not make 4. If you decide to move one man, he would have to stop first at 3 or at 1, before making the final move. Diagram 5 illustrates this rule. The black man cannot make a move of four, although the point is empty, because both his individual moves – one and three – are blocked (see page 16) by white pieces.

Hitting a blot

A "blot" is a single man occupying a point. A blot is unprotected and vulnerable to attacks by the other player (known as "hits" in the backgammon idiom). To hit a blot you must land, with one or more of your men, on its point. Then you put your opponent's man on the bar, that is on the space that divides the two tables in half. Diagram 6 shows two men hitting a blot, which is taken off the board and placed on the bar.

In diagram 7 overleaf a black man is on the bar. *The black player is not allowed to make any play before he re-enters the hit man in his opponent's inner table.* For this purpose each of the six points in the two inner tables has been given a number corresponding to the possible throws of a die, counting from the outside. Diagram 7 also shows the inner tables of both players. The white player's inner table has five of its six points blocked (see below, *Blocks*). Only one point – 4 – has been left vacant. The black player must throw a four and enter the hit man to the appropriate point, before being allowed to make any other moves.

Blocks

When two or more pieces of the same colour occupy a

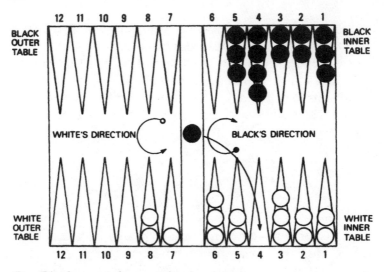

7. Black must throw a 4 to re-enter.

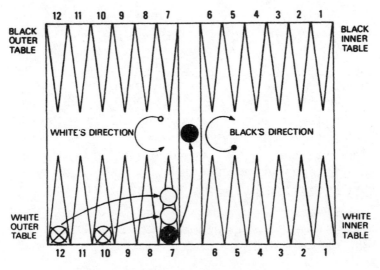

8. 5–3. Making a point and hitting a blot.

point ("make a point" in backgammon jargon), that point belongs to their side so long as at least two stay there, and constitutes a *block* for the opponent, who can neither land nor stop on it.

"Making points" is one of the most rewarding tactics in backgammon. Diagram 8 shows the making of a point and simultaneous hitting of a blot, by a play of 5-3.

Bearing off

Bearing off – that is, taking your pieces off the board – is the last phase of the game.

To bear off, all your men must first be in your inner table. You bear off in accordance with dice rolls. The six faces of a die correspond with the six points of your inner table (or that of your opponent's, if you have to re-enter a hit blot).

You must play your *entire roll*, if possible, even if this is to your disadvantage. Suppose that, when bearing off, the number on one of the dice relates to a point that is vacant. In this case, you have either to move a man within your table or bear off a man from a lower numbered point. For example, if you have your last two men on point one, and you throw 4–3, you bear off both of them, for they are on a lower number than your roll and no other men are on higher points. But if you have two men on point five and throw 4–3, you must move one man to point one and one to point two. You cannot bear any off.

A beginner asked me once: "Is it necessary always to apply the larger figure of the dice roll to the man who is further away from the end?

"For instance, if I have men on 4 and 5, and roll 6–3, do I have a choice of leaving a man either on 1 or on 2? Or *must* I apply the 6 to the man on 5 and be forced to leave the man on 1?"

"You are free to choose your priorities," I told him. "If

you *choose* to play 6 first – and 6 is a vacant point – you *must* bear off the man on 5. On the other hand, if you choose to play 3 first, you may move either man three points and then apply your 6 to bear off the man who is on the higher point.

"In other words, you *may* choose which figure you play first, but you *may not* choose from where to bear off a man, if a point is vacant. You must always bear off from the HIGHEST OCCUPIED POINT."

See Diagram 9.

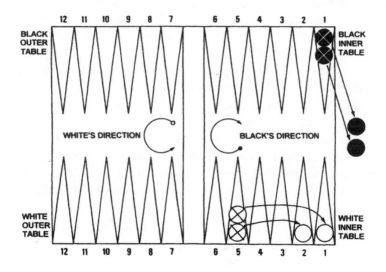

9. 4–3. Black (top) is able to bear off, but white (bottom) must move his men inside his inner table.

Even if you have only one man left, you may be unable to bear him off in certain circumstances. If your man is at six (Diagram 10) and you throw 4–1, no matter which move you make first, you are unable to bear him off.

Occasionally, your opponent may have left a block inside your inner table – two men occupying the same point – in the

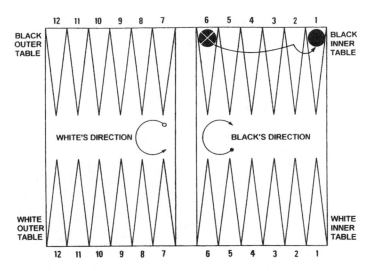

10.   4–1. Black cannot bear off.

hope that he may frustrate you at the eleventh hour (see Chapter 3, *Elementary Strategy*, page 26). This may prevent you from bearing off your pieces and sometimes may cost you the game.

In Diagram 11 the black player has two men on point 2 of your inner table. You have only two men left, one on point 5, one on point 4. You roll 5–2. You bear off your man on 5, but you are unable to bear off or move the man on 4. You are left with an exposed blot. Your opponent needs a 2 (or 1–1) to hit it.

You may play it differently. You may move, for instance, your man on 5 two points to 3, and then bear off the man on 4. This will leave you with an exposed blot again, but closer to your opponent's pieces and thus giving him fewer chances to hit it. For an explanation of this, see *Probabilities* (page 50).

22

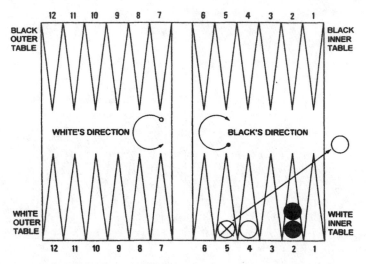

11. 5–2. White bears off 5, but he cannot move 2.

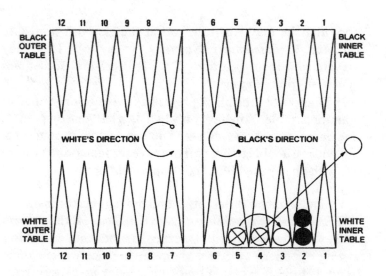

12. 5–2. A better way to play it.

Primes

Each point you make increases your chance of beating your opponent. Six points in a row constitute a *prime*. Since the dice have no number higher than 6, a prime is an impregnable wall against your opponent's men. It is one of the most important factors in the game, and when it is built in your inner table, the latter is called a *closed board*.

Victories

You win if you are first to bear all your men off the board.

There are three possible victories: single, gammon and backgammon.

A *single* victory is scored when your opponent has entered all his men in his inner board and has borne off at least one man.

A *gammon* or double victory is scored when your opponent has been unable to bear off any of his men.

A *backgammon* or triple victory is scored when your opponent has not taken off any men *and* has one or more of his men in your inner table.

Many discriminating players believe that "triple" victory or backgammon can only be achieved by scandalous luck and consequently should be abolished. We shall discuss this point later.

Summary of the rules

So far we have mentioned the basic rules of the game only. There are many other rules which regulate the gambling aspects of the game, such as the use of the doubling cube. These will be dealt with separately under *Gambling*.

Here is a summary of the basic rules:

— Backgammon is a game for two, combining skill and luck. (For a version for three to six players, see *Chouette*, page 48.)

· — It is played on a special board with twenty-four points. Each player has fifteen men and two dice.

— The object is to bring all your men into your inner board and then bear them off. The player who bears off his men first is the winner.

— The moves are regulated by dice. Dice also decide who plays first.

— Plays must be made for both dice, if possible. You may not refuse to make a move if one is possible. (There is no top limit on the number of men of the same colour that may occupy a single point).

— If you cannot make both moves – and you have a choice – the higher figure must be played.

— Each player must throw his dice into the board on his right. While he is moving his men, the dice must be left on the board. If a die falls outside or ends in a tilted position, the player must throw both dice again.

— At the start of a game either player may demand to use the same dice as his opponent, or to have the dice mixed.

— When you hit a blot, your opponent must make no move before re-introducing the hit man into your inner table.

— The points of the inner tables are notionally numbered from one to six. This enables the players to re-introduce their blots and bear off their men.

— Winner is the player who bears off all his men first. There are three types of victories: single, double (gammon) and triple (backgammon). Points are awarded according to your victory: one point for single, two points for double and three points for triple. There are proposals to abolish the triple (backgammon) victory.

— A friendly match is usually played over nine games: the first to win five is the winner. In this context a gammon victory counts as two games, and a backgammon as three towards the winning of five.

3

ELEMENTARY STRATEGY

No matter what tactics you may employ once you become a seasoned player, your overall strategy will always be prompted by two objectives:

— To move away your runners – that is, the two men in the inner table of your opponent.

— To prevent your opponent from moving his runners away.

It is best to do both at once, if possible. If not, you will have to choose either to attack, and risk losing a double game, or to block your opponent's runners by building as many obstacles in their way ("making points" in the backgammon idiom) as possible.

Some believe that adopting tactics is a matter of character rather than planning. Quite a few go even further by arguing that what we call "aggressive" or "defensive" attitudes are almost automatic, as they are chosen spontaneously by us. Yet one of the greatest assets of playing games is that they often force us to re-educate our instincts.

Players who always adopt aggressive, or defensive, attitudes, because "they cannot help it", rarely become masters in their games. The spontaneous reactions have to be deliberately checked in favour of a rational approach. Players must learn to assess the situation first, and then decide what type of game will enable them to achieve the best results. Needless to say, in the course of a game, they may have to change tactics more than once.

If that is "Greek" to the beginner, who is assumed to

know little more than how to move his men, take consolation in the fact that backgammon, like bridge, has many schools of play and various systems of evaluating a position.

Before going further on the subject of tactics, we need to understand that most analysts agree that the results of backgammon games are enormously influenced by dice rolls. Even the most expert players admit that skill does not contribute more than one quarter to the result of a game. The rest is luck. Skill in backgammon lies in adaptability to the whims of the dice – and knowledge of the probabilities.

Consequently, even an experienced player cannot decide beforehand what style of game he will adopt in a given contest, for it is the die that dictates both pace and style. All the same, *knowledge* of the available lines of play may enable him to choose the right one in the prevailing circumstances.

There are three sorts of games:
— Running.
— Back.
— Block or positional.

Another type of game, with its own pace and style, is gambling. This is described in Chapter 4 (page 40).

The beginner will be better equipped to appreciate the nuances of the game if he first understands the game's phases. So we give priority to the various stages before elaborating on the available styles.

The three phases of a game

There are three phases in each game: the opening moves, the middle game and the end game. On some occasions, the middle game is absorbed by the other two. It is, so to speak, squeezed between them, and so we go straight from the opening moves to the end game.

Each phase has its own strategy, formulated by vast experience which has been accumulated through centuries of playing. They therefore merit close examination.

(a) Opening moves

From the very beginning, the underlying principle is to "make" as many points as you can. The more points you make, the more obstacles you put in your opponent's way, for your blockade restricts his moves. Although a controlled point is valuable anywhere on the board, there are some particular points that should be given priority. It is worth taking risks to occupy them. Diagram 13 shows these points.

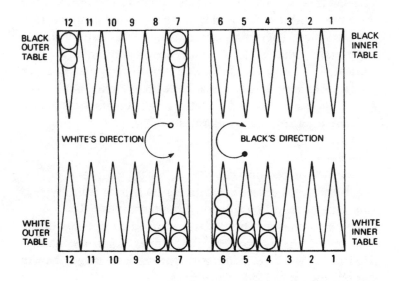

13. The vital points for white. Opposite them are black's vital points.

From the initial position, any one of these points *may* be occupied by a single throw – some in more than one way. For instance, point 5, which is of great tactical importance, can be controlled by throws of 3–1, 3–3, or 1–1. However, if the dice are obstinate, it is worth first playing a single piece there, in spite of the obvious risk of the blot being hit and sending another of your men back into your opponent's inner table. But the chances are that you *will* be able to make that important point.

Your six and four points are also significant for sound development, and you should try to control them as early as possible, even if you have to risk your men.

Generally speaking, the modern school of backgammon thinks that a game that is "too safe" becomes unproductive and dull. Moreover, the chances of a safe game being demolished by unlucky dice rolls are about the same as misfortune in games where you occasionally take some calculated risks.

Let us make it clear, we are not advising the beginner to adopt reckless tactics by thoughtlessly putting his men at the mercy of his opponent. What we say is that it is worth taking chances within reason. And a chance worth taking is to occupy vital points (Diagram 13) by exposing, if necessary, single men.

Still, before making a potentially sacrificial move, you should assess the current significance of a given point, the probabilities of having your man hit and the conditions in the inner table of your opponent.

At this stage you will gain greatly in experience if you take out your backgammon board, arrange the men in their initial position, as in Diagram 2, and instead of rolling your dice, move your men, to what you see as best advantage, according to the following list of dice rolls:

6–5, 6–4, 6–3, 6–2, 6–1
5–4, 5–3, 5–2, 5–1
4–3, 4–2, 4–1
3–2, 3–1
2–1

Each time you make a move, turn over the page and check it with table 1, which is in fact a complete list of all the possible dice rolls with the recommended or comparatively harmless first moves.

Table 1.

OPENING MOVES FOR WHITE

In standard backgammon you cannot start with a double. All the other possible throws are listed below, with recommended moves.

6-5 *'The lover's leap'*. B1 to B12.
6-4 B1 to B11.
6-3 B1 to B7 and B12 to W10. Or B1 to B10.
6-2 B1 to B9. Or B12 to W5.
6-1 B12 to W7 and W8 to W7. *'Making your bar point'*.
5-4 B12 to W8 and B12 to W9. Or B12 to W9 and B1 to B5. Or B1 to B10.
5-3 W8 to W3 and W6 to W3. *'Making your three point'*. Or B12 to W5.
5-2 B12 to W8 and B12 to W11.
5-1 B12 to W8 and B1 to B2.
4-3 B12 to W9 and B12 to W10.
4-2 W8 to W4 and W6 to W4. *'Making your four point'*.
4-1 B12 to W9 and B1 to B2. Or B12 to W9 and W6 to W5.
3-2 B12 to W11 and B12 to W10.
3-1 W8 to W5 and W6 to W5. *'Making your five point'*.
2-1 B12 to W11 and B1 to B2. Or B12 to W11 and W6 to W5.

The second player's first moves are more or less identical, though they sometimes have to vary if the previous move has made them impossible. In such cases a player should use his initiative and avoid over-exposing his men.

Diagram 14 is an example of tactics in the very early stages. White's first roll was 2–1. Black followed with a double six, which put him in control of both 7 points. Now white rolls 6–1: an unlucky throw, in the circumstances. There are few moves available, most of them unjustifiably risky. He plays safe by leaving two blots, both beyond the

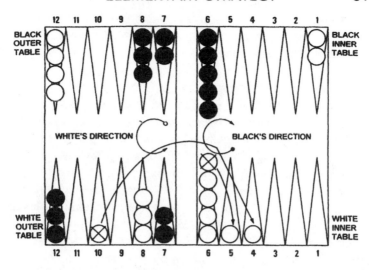

14. White 6–1. A harmless play.

reach of his opponent. Moving his "runner" from 1 to 2 would not give any advantage, while the chosen moves lay the foundation stones for a better protected inner table.

(b) The middle game

As in most other games, the middle game of backgammon is rich in variations – too rich to be codified – and relies heavily on the experience and talent of the players and, unless one is persistently lucky or unlucky, it is the decisive period of a game. One may roughly estimate that the results depend 40% on the middle game.

Yet we cannot define with certainty where the middle game starts and when it ends. Some players say that it starts approximately after the first five or six rolls. But seasoned tournament players argue that the number of rolls is irrelevant. The middle game, they claim, is a matter of position rather than the elapsed number of dice rolls. When you reach a position that a hit blot is likely to determine the result – then you know you are in the middle game. It ends when the first man is borne off the board or when no clash is possible, as in a running game.

(c) End game and bearing off

There is not much skill involved in the end game. What you have to do when all your men are safe and dry in your inner table is to bear them off in the fewest possible rolls.

But there are right plays and wrong plays. By a wrong play you may lose a game, which an experienced player would have won with the same dice rolls! Practice is necessary, even if you are destined to become a master tournament player!

As soon as your men are disengaged (i.e. have got past your opponent's men), the most important thing is to bring them to the inner table and start bearing off. As your opponent's pieces are out of the way, you do not have to take the usual precautions. There is no need to avoid exposing blots, which, in the previous two phases of the game, were vulnerable. What matters is to run faster than your opponent.

Two principles apply in this final phase of a game:

— Do not attempt to distribute your men evenly in the inner table. Just try to bring them in. Uneven distribution does not lose games.

— When you bear off, you should choose, whenever possible, to take a man off the board rather than to move one within your inner table.

Who knows? Your next roll might be the luckiest of the game. Showing foresight and taking precautions is good in the opening stages and mainly in the middle game. But in the end game you are at the mercy of the dice. They may be unpredictable, but not always bad!

Trapped men

Most end games are played when the men are disengaged. But on some occasions, your opponent may have left one or two of his men 'imprisoned' in your inner table. The trapped men may harass you while you are bearing off. Sometimes, a player may feel that he has lost his game and decides, as a last resort, to adopt a waiting game. See *Back Game* (page 36) for more details.

Diagram 15 shows a typical position of a sort of back game. Two hostile men are in your inner table. Your

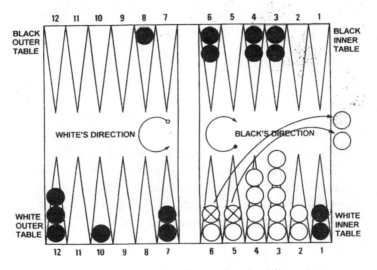

15.   A sort of *backgame*. A 6–5 may force white to leave two blots exposed.

opponent will try to leave them there as long as possible. He is lurking for the opportunity to hit one or two of your men and thus improve his lot.

A basic tactical precaution against this is to move your men within the inner table instead of bearing them off. If you manage to gather your men in, say, two points, when they were initially spread in five, the chances of leaving a blot exposed are drastically reduced. Another way to face the threat is to distribute your men evenly with each point holding an even number – two or four. This generally works, although occasionally it can prove disastrous. Imagine the catastrophe if you rolled 6–5 (Diagram 15). You have to expose two blots! Then the odds are very much in favour of your opponent. See *Probabilities*, page 50.

The three tactical games

To start with, a beginner may not be able to adopt any tactics at all. He will simply roll the dice and play what is in sight. Experience and advice will help him to see that by adopting a vague plan or some form of tactics he may increase his chances. And gradually he should develop ideas of his exact objectives in each phase.

There are three main tactical lines that you may adopt. Running, back, and positional or block. You cannot decide in advance what the type of game will be. This is beyond your control. It depends on the rolls of the dice and the moves of your opponent. You should be able, though, to adapt yourself to the conditions of a game. The ultimate aim is to win, and winning becomes easier with a plan.

Running game

The running game may be described as a competitive race, in which your sole aim is to bring your men, as fast as possible, into your inner table and bear them off. You do not have to take the usual precautions of even distribution or avoiding exposure of blots. The two racing teams become disengaged and now all depends on your position in relation to your inner table – and of course your dice rolls. As the latter are unpredictable, you must assess the situation before adopting a running game.

In fact, a running game is not adopted the moment the two sides are disengaged. This is poor tactics. *A running game is foreseen*. It usually starts after a short and mostly uneventful middle game. If there are no blots, which keep the two sides engaged, and the men are well protected in their points, you should evaluate the position and decide for or against a running game.

Usually you should know at a glance whether it is to your advantage to go for a running game. First, you check the inner tables: how many of your men are in your inner table and how many of your opponent's are in his. If he has two or three more men in his inner table and they are evenly distributed on the points, you should avoid a running game.

You must also check the outer tables. You do not have to count only the men, but also their distance from your inner table. See diagram 16. If you cannot assess the situation at a glance, and you prefer to count, there is a simple method

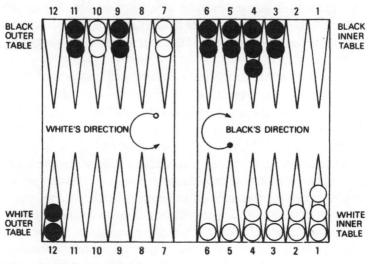

16. Counting a position.

advised by all the experts. Count the distance (in points) of each man from your sixth point – and add up the numbers.

In diagram 16 the position in the inner tables favours the white player, while the position in the outer tables slightly favours the black player. So either may opt for a running game, depending on who plays first. When the chances are even, the one whose turn it is to move has a small advantage.

The above position is fairly obvious. But you must learn to see through more complicated positions, and opt for a running game when this has some chance of success.

Back game

The back game is not a single form of game. There are two other similar games, that look deceptively like back games, but are not. Experts call them "semi-back" game and "nothing" or "trouble" game.

Let us first examine the proper or full back game. It is controlling two points in your opponent's inner board. If you hold his 1 and 3 points, or 1 and 2, you have achieved the ideal back game, as has white in diagram 17 opposite.

A semi-back game develops when you control one point only in your opponent's inner board. Ideally, this should be placed on the fourth point and thus threaten your opponent's blots.

Finally, the "nothing" or "trouble" game is a simulation of the back game, but lacking its threats and advantages. It all depends on the conditions in your inner table. If your men are so advanced that they only occupy the last 2 or 3 points, why hit a blot? It can re-enter at once.

Back games are *caused*, not chosen. They are the end-products of blot-fighting games. Usually a point is so fiercely contested that, in the ensuing battles, there are a number of blots hit. If these blots manage to re-enter in the ideally situated points, we have a back game situation.

As an option, a player should not voluntarily choose a back game. It is better for him to be alert for any chance of a successful running game, or to resort to a positional game, rather than to choose a back game. But if that sort of game is *imposed* by the circumstances, your object should be to hit any exposed blot on your way. For this reason, you should try to hold at least five points in your inner table. Otherwise, the back game is liable to backfire, and you may have to pay dearly for your choice.

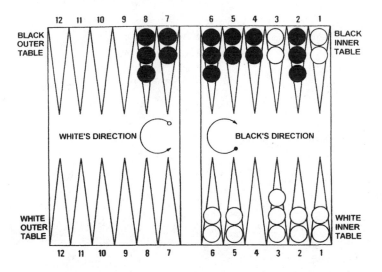

17.　Full back game.

Diagram 17 shows the ideal position of the white men in the black's inner table. Yet, white still needs low dice rolls to maintain his inner board as perfectly arranged as it is now. This game will eventually develop into one of endurance and slow pace rather than a race. If black does not expose a blot, white may be forced gradually to gather his men in the first three or two points, and thus transform an ideal back game to a "trouble" game.

Positional or blocking game

The more points you control, the better your chances of victory. Unlike the running and the back games, playing for positional advantage is more of a style than a strategy. Diagram 18 shows that making a point is often preferable to hitting a blot.

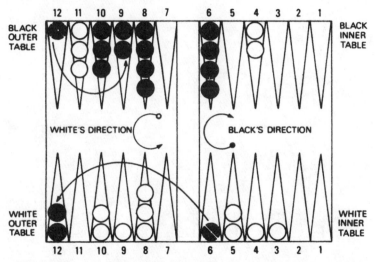

18.   Black 6–3. It is often preferable to "make points" than hit blots. Here, black removes his vulnerable blots on W6, W12, B12 and B9. Hitting the white blot on W9 would serve no useful purpose and leave black dangerously exposed.

Positional games are not played on inflexible principles or pre-conceived conditions. Their greatest assest is their adaptability as regards the position of the men and the throws of the dice. They are as versatile as backgammon itself. For this reason alone, one may describe them only in general and vague terms.

The one principle that stands out is:

"CONTROL AS MANY POINTS AS POSSIBLE."

Only experience and some knowledge of the probabilities will enable you to see through a given position and choose the right play.

4

GAMBLING

The mechanics of betting

Gambling is inherent in backgammon. There are more stories about financial catastrophes, fortunes that changed hands, wives sold, cheating and suicides than there are rules and instructions on play. During and after the Middle Ages, state and church joined in a desperate attempt to restrain players from losing vast amounts of money in backgammon, but their combined efforts came to nil. It seems that "the bug of gambling" has developed complete immunity from the various forms of advice and exhortation.

In brief, the apology for gambling is that it satisfies an ingrained need of the social being to improve his lot by taking calculated – and not so calculated – risks. The subject is vast and well beyond the scope of this book.

On the other hand, backgammon and the whole tables family would not have survived without the "obverse" side of the coin, which is the sheer pleasure derived from playing a game combining skill and luck in almost ideal proportions.

In previous chapters, we had a glimpse of the "innocent" aspects of the game: the rules, and how to play it well. Now we shall try to complete the picture by pinpointing the traps and helping the beginner to avoid them.

For one thing, betting is not necessarily gambling. It depends on the frequency and the scale. In Western Europe there is a widespread notion that backgammon is the game of the affluent classes. This is only partly true. Backgammon is a classless game. Its association with the affluent is due to the fact that their habits are better monitored than those of all the other classes put together. In Southern Europe and the Middle East, backgammon is not only highly popular but equally loved by rich and poor alike. No one ever attempted to associate it with gambling. In the eyes of the law and the conscience of the people, it is not a gambling game like Poker. A typical bet is playing for your opponent's coffee, in the same way that chess or draughts – games of pure skill – may be played for a cup of coffee. It is a "fee" paid to the better player rather than a bet.

The doubling cube

Before the introduction of the doubling cube, a player could lose one, two, or at most three points in a single game, depending on the position of his men when his opponent had borne off all his pieces. The doubling cube (an oversize dice bearing on its sides the arabic numbers 2, 4, 8, 16, 32 and 64) caused a radical change. And 64 is not the highest possible number! You could go on doubling and re-doubling indefinitely, beyond the 64. The numbers on the doubling cube represent points. So in a single game you could lose any number of points.

Some say that the doubling cube "pepped up" the pace of the game, for it enabled the players to resign and start a new game. It is, however, undeniable that it also made backgammon a gambler's paradise.

Let us see, first, how the doubling cube is used.

When a game starts, the doubling cube is placed with the 64 face up in the middle of the bar. This means that the game is still being played on single stakes. Doubling may be started by either player and may be either "automatic" or "voluntary".

Automatic doubling

This is random and outside the will of the players. Sometimes it even starts before the actual game: when the players throw a single die to decide who will play first. If they roll the same number (two fours, for instance) the stakes are automatically doubled, and whenever the same double appears – and in some circles whenever *any* double appears – the doubling happens automatically!

Thankfully this convention is not a rule of the game and we recommend that you ask for clarification of this point before you sit down to play. Automatic doubling may push the stakes so high that both players may be unable to meet them! You should state that this is *not* a rule of the game and anyway you do not play automatic doubling. If you have to make a concession, though, you may agree that you will accept *only one* automatic doubling, when the first double is rolled.

Voluntary doubling

This has become a part of the game and need not be restricted, within reasonable limits.

You may double when it is your turn to play and *before* you roll the dice. You should say "I double" and place the doubling cube on the bar, in front of your opponent, with the appropriate number up. For example, if you double first in a particular game, you should turn up 2, place it on the bar close to your opponent and wait for his answer.

If he says "I accept" the game continues with double stakes. If he says "no", the game is over and you win a *single* stake.

The most important rule of voluntary doubling, which makes it widely acceptable to the vast majority of backgammon players, is that once you double (or re-double) you have no right to double again until your opponent has done so. DOUBLING IS A RIGHT THAT ALTERNATES BETWEEN THE PLAYERS. This is a safety valve that should keep the gambling within reasonable limits.

.On the other hand, once you accept a doubling, you are not allowed to resign in the course of the game. You have to finish it, and if you lose it double or triple, you will have to pay the increased stakes multiplied by two or three, as the case may be.

For example, if the initial stake was one pound and you have increased it to two by doubling, you will have to multiply 2 by 2, if you lose a gammon, or 2 by 3, if you lose a backgammon.

Mastering the doubles

You should avoid playing with the doubling cube while you are still learning the game or when you play with persons unknown to you. It is wise to settle the following points before you start playing.

— You should make it clear that you do not play automatic doubles, as a matter of principle. Do not remain silent on this point, your opponent may claim that your silence represented agreement.

— In some clubs there are fixed stakes, which the old members may assume that you were aware of. Ask for the exact initial sum and make it clear this is not doubled automatically.

— You will have to accept the voluntary double, otherwise you would not find partners to play with. In some clubs they put a ceiling on the number of doubles. This is an additional protection against too high stakes. Whatever the case, since the right to double *alternates* between the contestants, you can keep the betting within reasonable limits. True, you need strong will and self-discipline to control your gambling instinct effectively. These are basic characteristics of good players. In fact, when they play among themselves the doubling cube very seldom goes above the mark 4. However, if the question of a limit is ever raised, you should readily accept it. Any compulsory limit that keeps betting to a low level should be welcome to the beginner. Misunderstanding may spoil a game and create an atmosphere of tension. To avoid this, you should always have the above points clarified.

A seasoned player identifies himself by the way he uses the doubling cube. For one thing, he never increases the stakes in order to intimidate his opponent out of an even game. And he doubles only when the odds are in his favour.

Experienced and master class players double only when:

— They count a position and find it to be at least 55/45% in their favour.
— They know the odds.

Doubling impulsively betrays inefficiency. It is an admission that one hopes to roll a double in the next few moves!

Counting a position

This is comparatively easy, and even a beginner can count a position with accuracy, provided that he knows *when* to do it. It is premature to count a position in the initial phase of a game, and often needless to do it when you are on the point of bearing off the last men.

You should count the position only when a game is about to become a running game. It is, in fact, a simple process. You count the number of points that separate a man from point 6 in your inner table, and then you add up the individual numbers. Then you do the same thing for your opponent's men. And finally you compare the two totals. The player with fewer points is better positioned.

No counting of a position is complete, unless you take into account the conditions prevailing in your inner table. You may not always need to count your men, but you should certainly check how they are deployed in it.

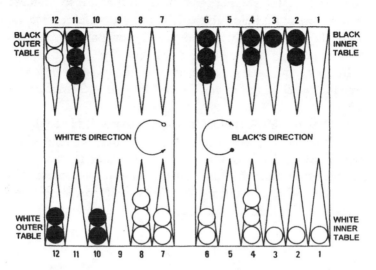

19. White should "double", if he can, before rolling the dice.

In Diagram 19 white is clearly better positioned than black. But the question is "is he so decisively better as to increase the stakes with confidence?" You have to compare the two totals and make up your mind. The answer is given below the diagram.

Knowing the odds

Knowing the odds in a given position is a more difficult task than counting. It requires experience. For one thing you have to be *selective*. You have to isolate the few men of both

sides who are relevant to your next move, and then you try to
assess the repercussions of your move. For example, if you
hit a blot, will you be able to protect your own man, who
may become a blot in his turn? And what is the situation in
your inner table? Are there any blots left there? If so what are
the chances of his being able to hit your blots and reverse the
odds? Is his inner table dominated, even partially, by his
own men?

In backgammon there are probabilities and miracles. You
should not rely on miracles. The odds against them are very
long.

In Diagram 20, it is black's turn to play 3–1. He could hit
the white blots at W9 and B11 – but what happens after-
wards? Black has a single man in his inner table, which
will become vulnerable, and white's inner table consists of a
good defensive formation. It is obviously preferable for
black to choose another move.

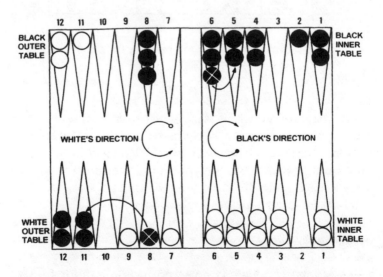

20.   Black 3–1. Black justifiably chooses to make points
rather than hit the blots at W9 and B11.

Playing for fun

Even before the introduction of the doubling cube, most of the problems were the same. For example, "should you hit a blot or not?" "If a blot is hit, what are its chances of re-entering the game quickly" and so on. These probabilities were not introduced or altered by the doubling cube. But the stakes were fixed beforehand, and the only way to double them was to win a double game.

The doubling cube added a new dimension to the game, but it also opened its doors to gamblers and alienated the amateur and family players, who enjoyed backgammon for its own sake or played it for trivial stakes.

The fact is that the doubling cube is here to stay. Thankfully for the many fans of the game, its effects can be easily checked, given self-discipline and choice of partners. For instance, you cannot possibly prevent your opponent from doubling, but you can stop him from increasing the stakes any further by refraining from re-doubling yourself. The rule is very clear on this.

No player is allowed to double twice in a row.
The right of doubling alternates.

Thus you can keep the stakes to a reasonable level and enjoy the game in its new dimension.

Another way to protect yourself from becoming the victim of unscrupulous gambling is to fix a top limit on betting. This may be arranged in various ways. The best, perhaps, is that each participant should be entitled to double *once only*. In practical terms this means that the initial stake can only be quadrupled as a maximum.

Whatever the private arrangements, a beginner should learn to play backgammon for fun. Small stakes admittedly make the game more attractive. But frequent and systematic gambling requires not only a good knowledge of the odds, but also persistent luck and the right temperament. What is more, as a profession it is rarely rewarding. Playing on equal terms in games of pure skill – like draughts or chess – is socially acceptable, for it involves a duel of skill and intellectual powers. But trying to earn one's living through a game which depends so much on dice rolls is not to be recommended.

On the other hand, backgammon is addictive. It may become an obsession. Therefore, its gambling side should be checked as early as possible. This is not only a personal view of the author. It is widely accepted and recommended by all the great masters and dedicated players. In tournaments, for example, there is a class for beginners, who are not allowed to use the doubling cube. It is considered too powerful for their class and experience.

Sooner or later, however, you will graduate to the doubling cube. Let us repeat, in brief, its main uses.

— *Automatic doubling.* In some schools, as soon as you roll an agreed double – and on some occasions any double – the stakes are automatically doubled. But I recommend you not to play under these conditions.

— *Voluntary doubling.* Provided that the players alternate in increasing the stakes, there is no other limit to stop them. In some places voluntary doubles are restricted – that is they cannot exceed a certain number.

The sole ally of the gambler, besides his lucky stars, is a good knowledge of the probabilities. See Chapter 5.

Chouette

This is a pure gambling game for three to six players. A beginner should not participate in a Chouette game, even if he knows the rules and has absorbed the elementary tactics. Chouette rules vary slightly from place to place and you should have them well and comprehensively explained before you participate.

We include it here for it is consistent with the objectives of this book to explain the mechanics of gambling, as the beginner of today will become the mature player of tomorrow.

The rules of Chouette are, in brief, as follows:

— This is a game designed for three to six players.

— The participants throw a die to arrange their priority.

— The first player, called THE MAN IN THE BOX, plays against all the other players, who form a team.

— The second player, THE CAPTAIN, is the leader of the team. He may consult the others in the course of a game, but he is entitled to play as he thinks proper, if there is no unanimity.

— In doubling, if all the other players oppose the increase of the stake, he has to bow to the decision. If the players are split, he may proceed as he likes. Players who disagree with his decision may resign.

– The right to resign makes it necessary for the score-keeper to keep a separate account for each player.

– If the man in the box loses, he is replaced by the captain.

– The man in the box may lose or win as many times his initial stake as the number of players in the team.

Putting aside its gambling overtones, Chouette is a pleasant alternative to regular backgammon.

5

PROBABILITIES

Hitting blots

Probability is the solid ground on which both tactics and strategy of backgammon are based. It may be called the prosaic heart of a poetic game. It is the infrastructure of backgammon. Yet you may still win if you ignore the exact numbers. You do not have to know that the odds against

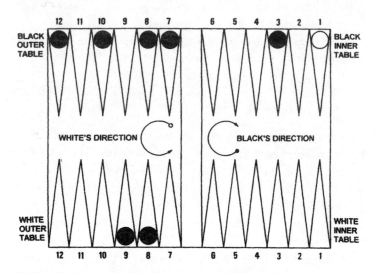

21. A blot in a direct reach distance (1–6) is more vulnerable than one further away. White B1 needs a 6–5 to hit B12; 5–5 to hit W9 and 4–4 to hit W8. The odds against are very long.

hitting a blot which is eleven points away from your nearest man are 1 in 17. You may express it in another way. You may say "that is a long shot" – and the effect will be the same.

There are tables, compiled by statisticians, which give you, in exact numbers, the for and against odds in a given position. But the beginner may be confused rather than helped by reading long lists of numbers, which he can neither memorise nor understand. Nonetheless, for those who want to know the arithmetic of the game, we incorporate the basic data at the end of this chapter (page 55).

Now look at Diagram 21. We purposely left only a few men on the board, all of them potential blots, to enable you to grasp *instinctively* the essence of probabilities. There is only one white man and a handful of black men. The first truth is:

It is easier to hit a blot which is six or fewer points away, than a blot which is seven or more points away.

The reason is simple: you can reach a man up to six points with one die only, but you can never reach seven points with one die. You have to use a second die to reach seven points or more. To roll a seven, you must rely on a combination of two dice. There are plenty. 6–1, 5–2, 4–3. But there are also plenty of combinations to roll a six. 5–1, 4–2, 3–3, 2–2, *and* any combination with a six in it. So you do not have to learn a number by heart. You can guess that it is easier to hit a six than a seven. And when you *do* have to expose a blot, you will know which is the better distance.

In Diagram 21, the two black men on B7 and B8 are six and seven points, respectively, away from your man. If you take a pair of dice and start rolling, you may get a seven with your first throw – or take twenty throws before you roll a six. Never mind! This does not change the principle – nor the odds. Despite the occasional whims of the dice, if you must expose a blot, *seven points are better than six*. At seven points away, your chances of being hit are fewer.

Now let us turn again to the same diagram. There is a blot even nearer than six, just two points away. Is it theoretically easier to hit a two than a six? The answer is an emphatic NO.

A two is a *direct roll*. A direct roll is one that can be done with one die. An *indirect roll* is one that requires two dice – that is, a seven or higher. Any distance between six and one is a direct hit distance. And any distance from seven upwards is an indirect hit distance.

So let us first take a closer look at the direct hit distances. The highest number, six, is also the most vulnerable. The lowest number, one, is the least vulnerable. And the risk increases with each number. So a three is less vulnerable than a six, but more vulnerable than one or two. Thus the second truth is:

If you must expose a blot to a direct throw (1–6), put it as close to your opponent's men as possible.

The indirect throws work on the opposite principle. Seven is the most vulnerable distance. The longer the distance, the less the risk.

It is better to expose your blots to an indirect hit than to a direct one. A nine-point distance is safer than a three-point distance.

So much about the probabilities of hitting a blot.

Re-entering blots

When the inevitable happens – and it happens too often in backgammon – and you have one or two men on the bar, your problem will be how to enter them back on the board, that is in your opponent's inner table. Remember that no other move is allowed before re-entering any hit men.

The odds against re-entering a man from the bar depend entirely on the number of points occupied by your opponent's men in his inner table.

So if your opponent occupies ("has made" in back-gammon jargon) five points, your chances are very low. If one point only, your chances are very high.

Now have a look at Diagram 22. There are two blots, one black and one white, facing each other at a distance of six points. Let us assume that it is white's turn to play and that he rolls a six. The first reaction of the beginner is "I'll hit!" The seasoned player, however, has other things to take into consideration before hitting.

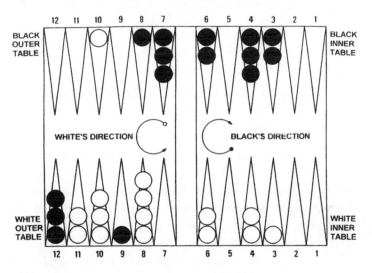

22. If white is to play he should not hit the black blot at W9. If it is black's turn, he may well hit and make a point at B8.

One thing is the position in his own inner table. White occupies two points and has one man exposed. So the blow against the black would not be a catastrophe. What is more, black may hit the exposed man when he re-enters.

On the other hand, with three points occupied in his inner table, plus the bar point (B7), black is somewhat stronger than white. If the game develops into a *fight of blots*, black's chances are better than white's.

Finally, white has to check the general position on the board. The outer tables favour black who also has more pieces in his inner board. So white's chances are not all that good anyway. By hitting a blot now, he is inviting black to hit back and possibly win. It is better for white to play his six elsewhere. There is no exact scientific formula covering cases of this kind. Experience – and instinct, born of experience – will teach you when and how to assess tricky positions.

Make sure you do not hit a blot just for the sake of it. You have to take into consideration all the other factors. But often it is advisable to hit if the position does not favour you.

Odds for making a point

If there is already a blot on a point, the odds of making a point out of it are the same as the odds for hitting a blot.

If you need to move two men to make a point (for example a 4–2), the odds against are very long. Dice are idiosyncratic and stubborn. What is more, they have no memory. They may keep on showing the wrong numbers until a player's patience is exhausted.

The best way to occupy a point is to move a blot at it and then try "to make it", as you would have tried to hit a blot. True, leaving a blot is not safe, but chances have to be taken.

The odds

For the benefit of readers with an interest in the arithmetical basis of probability, I give below the calculation of the odds of hitting a blot (or making a point) and of re-entering the board (coming back).

For a throw of two dice, each die can fall showing any one of six different numbers, a total of $6 \times 6 = 36$ possible combinations. as follows:

1–1	2–1	3–1	4–1	5–1	6–1
1–2	2–2	3–2	4–2	5–2	6–2
1–3	2–3	3–3	4–3	5–3	6–3
1–4	2–4	3–4	4–4	5–4	6–4
1–5	2–5	3–5	4–5	5–5	6–5
1–6	2–6	3–6	4–6	5–6	6–6

The chances of hitting any particular blot (disregarding the question of whether intermediate occupied points could interfere) can be calculated by counting how many of the combinations from the above table would succeed, dividing that number by the total possible number of combinations (36) and expressing the result as a percentage, as shown in Table 2.

Working out the chances of bringing one man back from the bar (re-entering) is a calculation of a different kind. Here it does not matter *which* points are available, only how many. The most straightforward way is to work out how many of the 36 possible combinations would *fail*, and from this derive the number that would succeed. The latter figure, divided by 36 and expressed as a percentage, gives you the percentage chance of succeeding.

This is all shown in Table 3 which also illustrates the generality that the chance of having one of the two dice come up with any individual number is 31%. If you have a choice from two numbers, the chance is 56%, and so on.

Table 2. Hitting a blot.

DISTANCE	COMBINATIONS	NUMBER OF SUCCESSFUL COMBINATIONS	SUCCESSFUL CHANCES % (to nearest 1%)
1	1-1, 1-2, 1-3, 1-4, 1-5, 1-6, 2-1, 3-1, 4-1, 5-1, 6-1	11÷36	31
2	2-1, 2-2, 2-3, 2-4, 2-5, 2-6, 1-2, 3-2, 4-2, 5-2, 6-2, 1-1	12÷36	33
3	3-1, 3-2, 3-3, 3-4, 3-5, 3-6, 1-3, 2-3, 4-3, 5-3, 6-3, 1-2, 2-1, 1-1	14÷36	39
4	4-1, 4-2, 4-3, 4-4, 4-5, 4-6, 1-4, 2-4, 3-4, 5-4, 6-4, 1-3, 3-1, 2-2, 1-1	15÷36	42
5	5-1, 5-2, 5-3, 5-4, 5-5, 5-6, 1-5, 2-5, 3-5, 4-5, 6-5, 1-4, 4-1, 2-3, 3-2	15÷36	42
6	6-1, 6-2, 6-3, 6-4, 6-5, 6-6, 1-6, 2-6, 3-6, 4-6, 5-6, 1-5, 5-1, 2-4, 4-2 3-3, 2-2	17÷36	47
7	1-6, 6-1, 2-5, 5-2, 3-4, 4-3	6÷36	17
8	2-6, 6-2, 3-5, 5-3, 4-4, 2-2	6÷36	17
9	3-6, 6-3, 4-5, 5-4, 3-3,	5÷36	14
10	4-6, 6-4, 5-5	3÷36	8
11	5-6, 6-5	2÷36	6
12	6-6, 4-4, 3-3	3÷36	8

There is also a theoretical 1 in 36 chance (3%) of hitting certain higher numbers with doubles, i.e. 15 (5-5), 16 (4-4), 18 (6-6) and 20 (5-5).

The same chances apply when one man has to be moved to "make" a point.

Table 3. Coming back from the bar.

POINTS OPEN	HOW MANY THROWS FAIL	HOW MANY SUCCEED	CHANCES OF SUCCESS %
5	1	35	97
4	4	32	89
3	9	27	75
2	16	20	56
1	25	11	31

6

SAMPLE GAME

Although you should by now know something about the elementary strategy, the gambling systems and the dice odds, nothing replaces the experience derived from playing the game.

When you have to play an unfavourable dice roll within a few seconds, the theories and the systems evaporate – but not the practical things that you have learned by playing games.

The game that follows has been selected for its versatility. In the first phase it is played "safely" by both contestants, but it develops to fierce blot-fighting and is unexpectedly

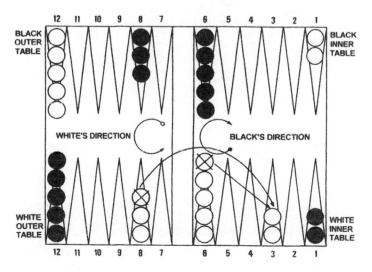

23. White 5–3. He makes his 3 point. A "safe" move.

won by the player who had been forced to adopt a back game.

You will be able to play it through easily, even without a backgammon set (though this is not recommended) for there is a diagram for each dice roll.

There are brief comments which either clarify or hint at the intentions of the players. When a move is given without comments, it means that it is a routine one.

As it benefits you to participate actively in the game, you will find at the end of some comments an asterisk (*). This means: "Should the player double (if permitted) before rolling the dice?" You will have to assess the position and answer yes, no or perhaps. Check your answers at the end of the chapter.

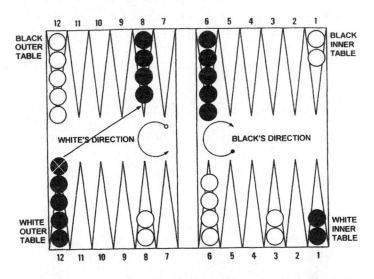

24. Black 3–2. Another "safe" move. Too safe for some experts, and not recommended on page 30.

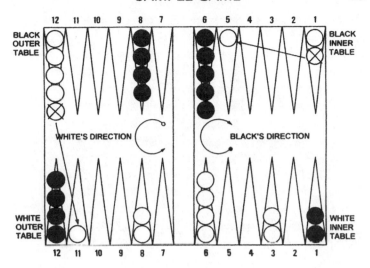

25. White 4–2. The best in the circumstances, for he cannot make his 4 point without leaving a blot at 8.

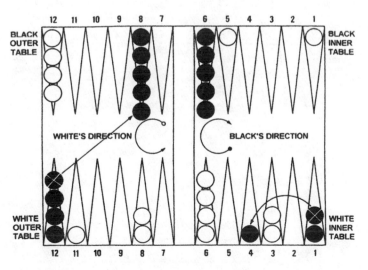

26. Black 5–3. His 3 point is not so urgent, for one of the white runners is already beyond it (B5).

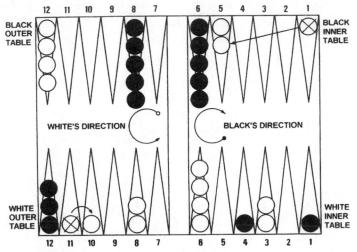

27. White 4–1. By moving to W10 he brings the black blot at W4 within range.

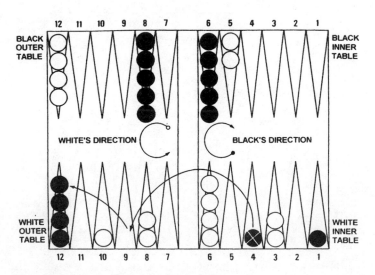

28. Black 5–3. One of many options.

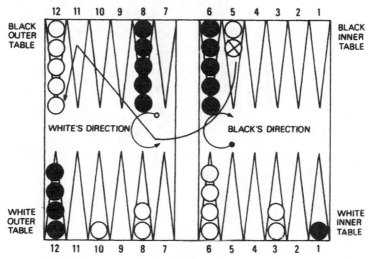

29. White 6–1. B5 to B12 preferred to the safer move W10–W3. He prepares for a *running* game.

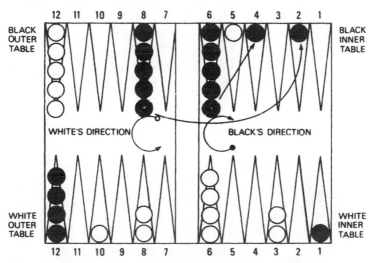

30. Black 6–2. W1 to W9 might prove too risky.

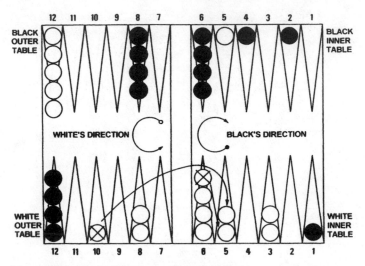

31. White 5–1. He makes his 5 point.

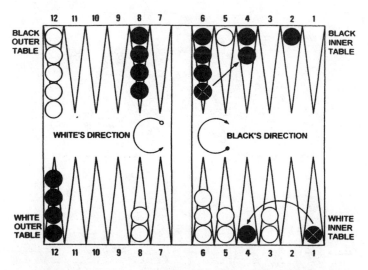

32. Black 3–2. He advances "the runner" and "makes" his 4 point.

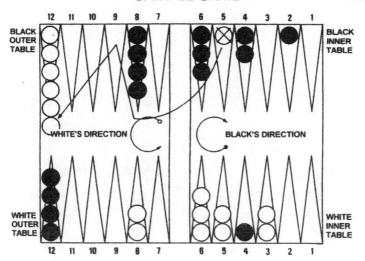

33. White 4–3. He seems to go for a "running game", for he has a slight advantage.

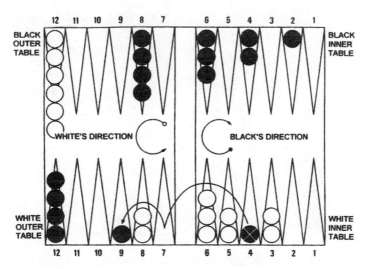

34. Black 3–2. Reducing the odds of being hit.

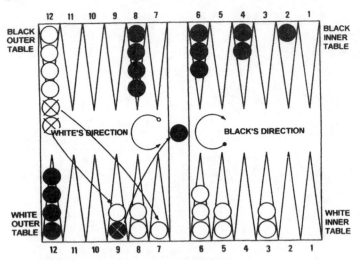

35.   Should white double before rolling?* (See notes at the end of the game.) White 6–4. He hits the blot at W9 and instead of advancing to W3, he exposes another blot at W7. Too risky, but could prove rewarding.

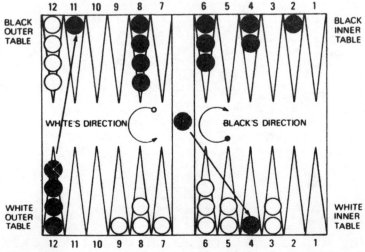

36.   Black 4–2. Re-introduces the blot at 4 and plays 2 elsewhere.

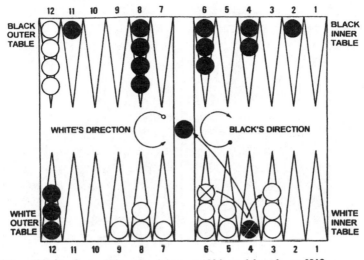

37. White 2–1. Hits the blot at W4 and lands at W3.

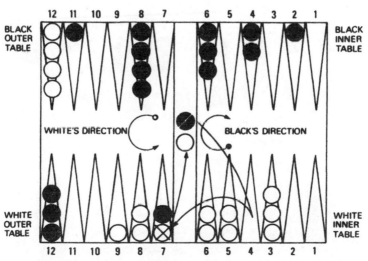

38. Black 4–3. Re-enters at 4 and hits with 3. Black was in a poor position so takes chances. This move initiates the "battle of blots" that will follow.

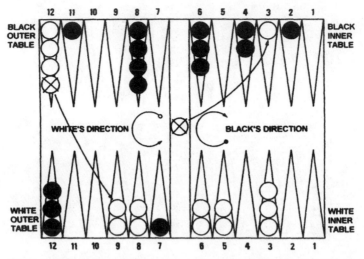

39. White 3–4. Re-enters at 3, makes his 9 point with 4.

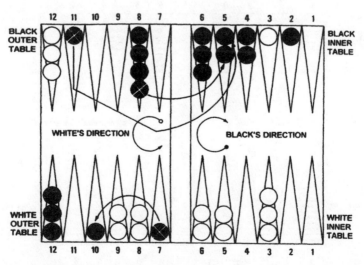

40. Black 3–3. Makes his 5 point and advances his back "runner" to W10.

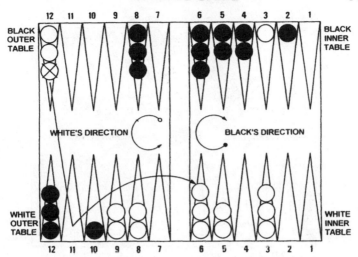

41.   White 5–2. Unable to run away from the black's inner table or to hit a blot, he advances his B12 to W6.

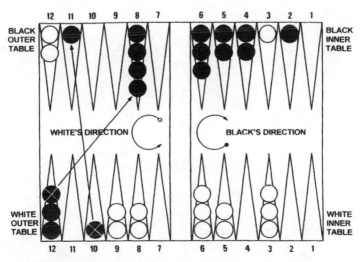

42.   Black 5–4. The odds against white hitting the blot at B11 are very long.

68

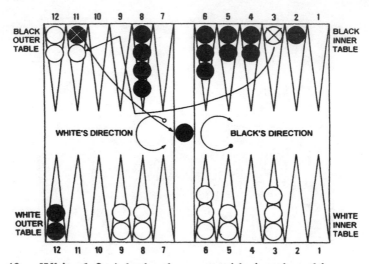

43. White 6–2. A lucky throw considering the odds.

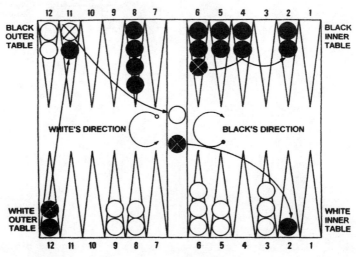

44. Black 2–2. Another lucky roll!

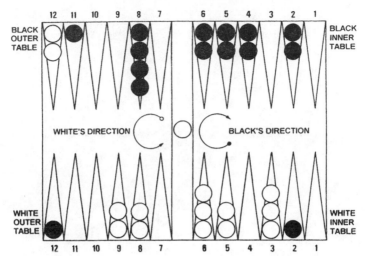

45. White 5–4. He cannot re-enter the hit blot, and consequently he cannot move.

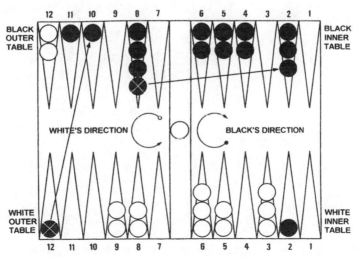

46. Black 6–3. Good in the circumstances.

70

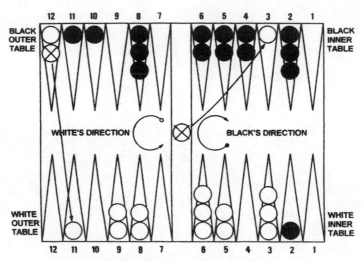

47.   White 3–2. Re-enters but cannot escape.

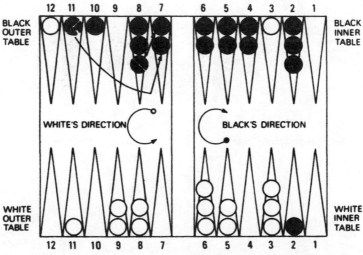

48.   Black 4–1. Makes the bar (7) point. Now black has five points in a row.

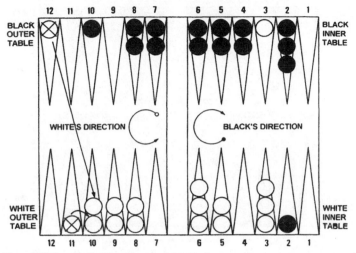

49. White 3–1. Makes his ten point.

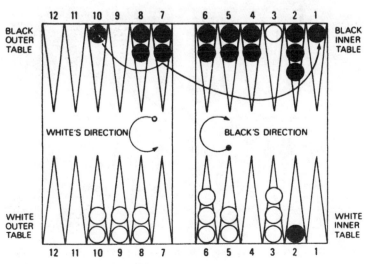

50. Black 6–3. He still cannot escape.

72

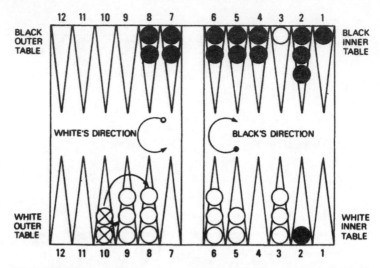

51. White 2-1. No escape possible, so he reinforces his 8 and 9 points.

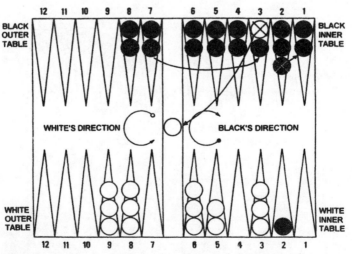

52. Should black double?* Black 4-1. Hits but exposes a blot on his inner table.

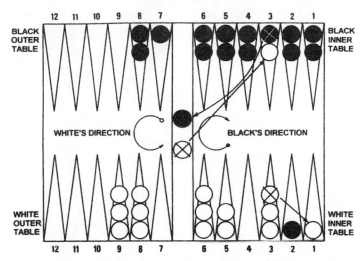

53.   White 3–2. Re-enters the board and hits, but the move to W1 is premature. From W8 to W6 would be preferable.

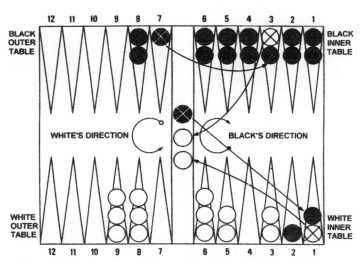

54.   Black 4–1. Re-enters and hits. The "battle of blots" is in full swing.

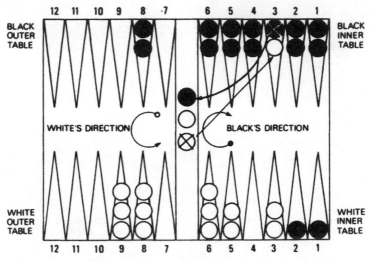

55. White 5–3. Only 3 is playable.

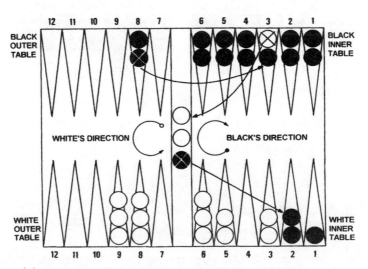

56. Should black double. if able?* Black 5–2.

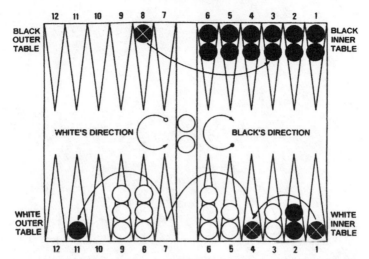

57. White 6–2. No possible move. Black 5–3. Closes the
board. White: no throw. Black 4–3. White: no throw.

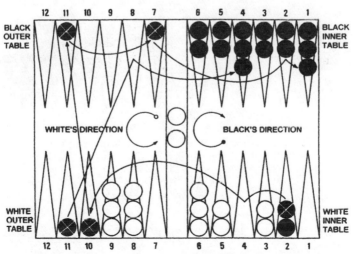

58. The position after several black moves. White is totally
immobilised.

76

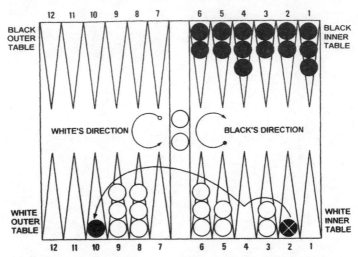

59.   Black 6–2. White's position is absolutely hopeless.

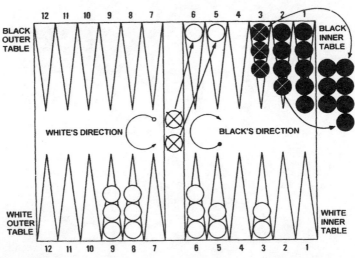

60.   Black 4–4, after several throws. White concedes a gammon (double) game.

Diagram 35:   Doubtful. His advantage is very slight.
Diagram 52:   Yes. The odds are in black's favour.
Diagram 56:   Yes. With five points in his home board, he *must*.

7

POSITIONAL STUDIES AND DOUBLING

Two games can never be the same

The game recorded in the previous chapter was chosen for its versatility, fast pace and suspense – qualities associated with backgammon, when played with intelligence and knowledge of the elementary tactics.

But one game cannot cover the whole subject. The greatest asset of backgammon is that in a whole lifetime, you never deal twice with *exactly* the same situations and problems. The variety and subtlety of the game are inexhaustible.

The middle game, in particular, can provide players with an astronomical number of variations, which it is impossible to codify. However, these variations can be classified in a comparatively few patterns.

In this chapter I shall deal with two separate subjects:

a)   The most representative patterns, i.e. those that occur more commonly.

b)   The "mirages", bluffs and the unsatisfactory rules concerning the use of the cube in competitions.

The subject of *representative patterns* lies on the border-line between elementary and advanced tactics, and it is possible that even the most intelligent *inexperienced* players may find them difficult to understand. I hope, however, that as soon as the beginner becomes a fully fledged player, he will come back to these pages, and will then be able to appreciate their implications.

The perils of the back game

I shall start with an analysis of an end game position. Despite their complexities, end games do not usually present the vast number of possible permutations seen in the middle games.

The reason that prompted me to choose a back game was the fact that, in the previous chapter, the winner was the player who successfully applied back game strategy. The result of that game may mislead the beginner, for a back game should be played only if *all the possibilities of other games have been closed.*

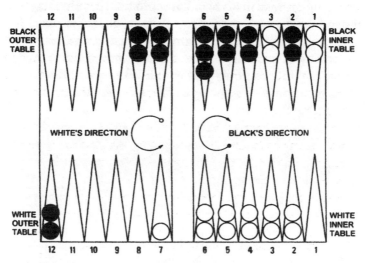

61.   A typical back game position.

A back game is normally a strategy of despair. Whoever adopts it – or rather is forced to adopt it – should have no chance of winning a conventional running or positional game.

Now look at Diagram 61. The arrangement of the men reminds us of a back game. White has four men in black's inner table and, on top of this, he also has a quite strong inner table of his own. Black, too, seems to be strong, although more of his men are dispersed in other tables. The position, by its nature, defies "counting".

White's hopes can only be realised if he manages to hit – as early as possible – one or more black men. Time is not on white's side, for he must retain the formation in his inner table. Black, on the other hand, hopes that the impeccable formation in white's inner table will soon collapse. When it does, he will not mind having one or two of his men hit, for he will be able to re-enter them soon and win.

The odds in black's favour are good. White has virtually no chance of winning. The reader can easily verify this by arranging the men in his backgammon board, as in Diagram 61, and start rolling the dice to make alternate plays for black and white until the game is decisively won by one player. Out of five games, four, at least, should end in favour of black. White can only win with a very lucky fall of dice.

The position after some dice rolls is shown in Diagram 62.

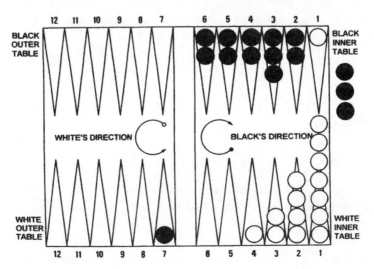

62. No chance at all for white.

White is virtually out of the game. The reason is simple: once his home board collapsed, he had no chance at all. This is the usual fate of back game players: on average they win only one out of five games.

Conflicting tactics

The arrangement of the men in Diagram 63 suggests a

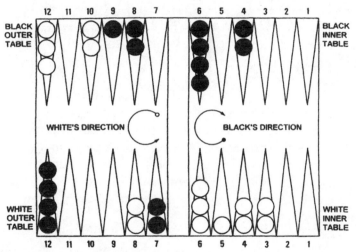

63.   Early middle game.

middle game. White may opt for a running game, since his position is somewhat better than black's. On the other hand, black would like to hold back for a while, in the hope that he would force white to expose a blot or two. So the objectives of the players conflict so far as the choice of tactics is concerned.

The dice rolls that followed did not seem to give advantage to either player. The situation remained little changed (Diagram 64). The desired "escape" to a running

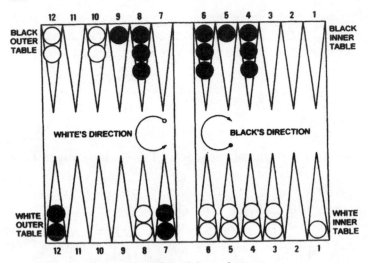

64. No breakthrough for either player.

game is virtually incapable of fulfilment. So both players have to revise their plans. White adopts a positional game, while black's development prompts him to adopt more aggressive tactics. After several rolls, in which white reinforced his defences, the game seemed to go in his favour, as in Diagram 65.

The lesson is that when players adopt different tactics – provided they are the right ones for a particular game – the one who manages to impose his strategy should eventually win.

The beginner must again be reminded that over 70% of the results depend on the fall of the dice. Very often, even the adoption of the right tactics does not lead to victory. The backgammon player should learn to be patient not only with the whims of his own dice, but also with the good fortune of his opponent's.

Luck has no rules, I am afraid. You cannot arrange for it to alternate like the doubling cube. All the same, *knowledge of the elementary tactics gives a decisive advantage.* Players

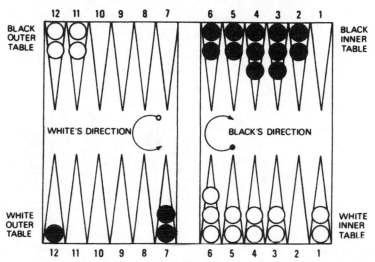

65.   White manages to improve his strategy. His position is more advantageous.

who defy or deliberately ignore tactics tend to lose twice as many games than those who adopt a strategy and are ready to revise it, should this become necessary.

The risks of doubling

Even the adversaries of the doubling cube admit that it is here to stay. The most serious risk – that it stresses the gambling aspects of the game – can be eliminated by sensible use. In Chapter 4 we discussed this in some detail and reached the conclusion that when the cube is used in moderation it is an advantage rather than a handicap.

The player whose turn it is to call the next double, at any stage of the game, has a slight extra advantage over his opponent. (This is an additional good reason why you should not use it too often.) This advantage becomes greater in the end game. And sometimes, in the last three or two dice rolls, you can take chances and increase your gains.

It is white's turn to play (Diagram 66). Both players are bearing off. White has three men left in his home board

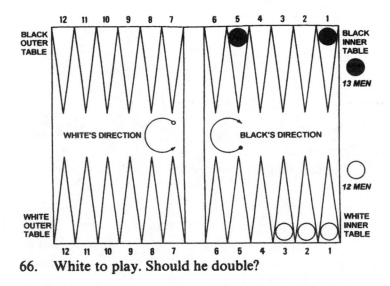

66. White to play. Should he double?

(another way to say "inner table"), black only two. White has to roll a double higher than 1–1 to win with his first throw. On the opposite side of the board, however, the black men are not ideally positioned. One is on point 5, the other on point 1. The chances for black to win on his next throw are rather better than 50/50.

White doubles before throwing the dice! Did he take a calculated risk? Should black accept the challenge? The answer to both questions is "yes".

White has taken a calculated risk. His men are better deployed in the inner table than those of black, but there are more of them.

On the other hand, white knows that unless black can throw a 5 or 6 (or 2–2, 3–3 or 4–4) he is unable to win in one move. So in spite of the odds (which at 55/45% are close but somewhat favour black), he offers to double. Black accepts. Both sides are sticking reasonably to the laws of probabilities. This is not reckless gambling.

Here is the exact arithmetic of the probabilities:

		WINS OUT OF 36
White's first throw	Five times out of 36, he will throw a double higher than 1–1, and win outright.	5W
Black's first throw	Of the 31 (out of 36 occasions) that black gets his first throw, he wins by bearing off both men on $^{23}/_{36}$ of the 31 occasions.	20B
White's second throw:	If black fails to bear off both men, white must succeed in bearing off all three men in two throws, even if he throws the worst possible 2–1, 2–1.	11W

So, out of each 36 occasions, black wins 20 times and white wins 16 times.

I do not urge the beginner to play against the probabilities, but the *last two rolls* in a game may be treated as an exceptional case, provided there is reasonable hope behind the doubling.

Psychological factors

In gambling, many other factors besides probabilities come into play. The psychological factor is one of the most important. It is used extensively in all sports and games where competition is fierce, although it is not universally considered to be "clean" or fair or even sportsmanlike. What matters, though, is that in most cases it proves very effective.

The psychological element is not a recent invention nor can it be analysed in simplified terms. Confidence – even if faked – is certainly an asset. Bluff – for instance, that you can afford to lose that amount – plays a decisive part. There are scores of things that can impress or – better still – intimidate your opponent into retreat. Economic "blackmailing", by raising the stakes, is also very effective.

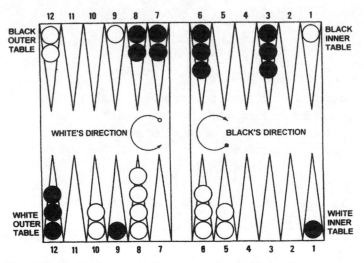

67.　Black doubles to 16. Economic "bullying".

In Diagram 67 the position of the pieces does not seem to favour any player. Yet black doubles to 16! Now white is faced with a stake which is too high for him and which he cannot afford to lose. So he does not accept the increase and loses eight times his initial stake. Cases like this one are frequent in gambling circles.

Economic "bullying" is one of the usual weapons of experienced gamblers against newcomers, though it cannot be used effectively against equally experienced players.

A novice who is introduced to a backgammon-playing circle, should make it clear that he will not *on principle* play the so-called automatic doubling. Secondly, he should overcome the temptation to double, even if the position favours him. This holds the professional gambler to a mere doubling of the stakes! The trick that a seasoned gambler may use is to offer incentives to his opponent to increase the stakes. He may even pretend to be bored to death without the war climate that a frequent raising of the stakes can create. So long as you are still a novice and uncertain, you should face the challenge with good humour and, mostly, with eloquent silence. True, you may lose some playing partners with these tactics, but you will maintain the right to go on playing a delightful game.

8

TOURNAMENTS

In clubs and places where players meet at regular intervals, a tournament is the most welcome event. If entry is restricted to the members of the club, it can be conducted under the same rules as the regular meetings. However, if members from other clubs are invited, it is necessary to organise the tournament on a more formal basis. You will have to state clearly:

What kind of tournament it is.
On which system it will be conducted.
What prizes will be given.
Who will referee it.

Types of tournament

A tournament may be local, national or even international. It also may be open – which means that everyone may apply to participate – or invitational. In invitational tournaments you undertake to invite players who are good enough to participate in it. In all cases, there should be a clear summary of the prevailing rules.

Unlike chess and bridge, the rules for backgammon tournaments vary from club to club and from area to area.

If there are a large number of participants, you should explain how and when the eliminating rounds will take place in order to reach the last eight or sixteen players. If more than sixteen players participate in the finals a tournament becomes chaotic.

When you advertise your tournament, you should ask the interested players to send a large self addressed envelope for the rules, the venue and the dates.

Prizes

There should not be money prizes, unless professionals participate. Between amateurs, book tokens or small gifts, like a small backgammon set, make the most popular awards.

Systems

If fewer than eight players participate, the best system is for each player to meet all the others in a series of pre-arranged contests. The winner is credited with one point. There are no points for the loser. When all the matches are completed, the player with the most points is the winner, or champion.

If there are sixteen players or more – the best system is the "knock out". The losers are out of the tournament and the winners play each other until a single champion is arrived at.

However, if the number of players is between eight and fourteen, the "Swiss System" is both fair and highly competitive. Its only disadvantage is that it may take some time.

In the Swiss System, a player who loses once is not out of the tournament. A player has *to lose twice* before being eliminated. Diagram 68 shows how this system works – though there can be variations in the details. The diagram is for eight players. There could be sixteen or even thirty-two – but then a tournament would last too long. If there are more than eight players – say eleven – you must eliminate the three surplus players. This is easy: you draw the names of six players by lot. These form a preliminary round of three pairs. The three losers are out of the finals.

90

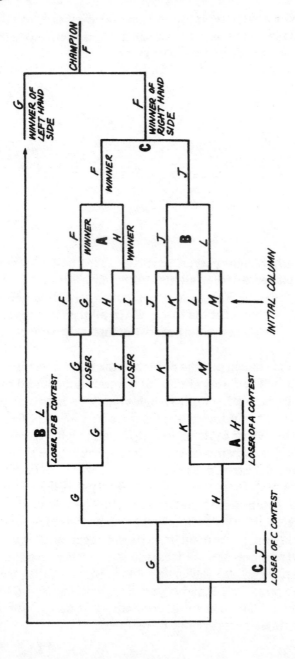

68. *"Swiss System"* (double defeat), for eight players. Can be doubled to sixteen, thirty-two, etc. No player is knocked out before losing two matches.

Under the Swiss System there is no need to seed the best two players. No matter how unfair the draw might be, the best two players will meet in the final.

The organisers write down the names of the participants in the (arrowed) initial column. The winners go on to the right; the losers to the left. A and B are the semi-final matches in the winners' column. C is the final match to decide the winner of the right-hand side. On the left-hand side you will find the same letters. These indicate the place to which the losers of the above contests are transferred. To decide the champion, the winner of the winners' side (right-hand) meets the winner of the losers' side.

This is the fairest "knock out" system that has been invented so far. But if more than sixteen players participate, it tends to become protracted and it is not recommended.

The rules must stipulate the number of points required for a player to win a match. In some tournaments, the winner is the player who first wins nine points, that is best of seventeen. But this is too much. Best of nine is a reasonable number to decide a match. Whoever first takes five, wins. Of course, the rules may stipulate that the final is best of fifteen.

The organisers must clarify whether the doubling cube will be allowed, and, if so, whether its use will be limited or unlimited. With an unlimited doubling cube, a whole match may be won in a single game!

Another point that must be clarified is whether gammons or backgammons (triple games) are acceptable. Many master players feel that if the cube is allowed, then neither double nor triple games should be counted as such; all the games should be considered as single ones, unless a player has used his cube. This rule allows the loser to reject the double game and thus lose only a single point.

In my judgment, the doubling cube is not compatible with the idea of a tournament and should be banned. A tournament should be conducted on traditional lines. Gammon and backgammon should count two and three points respectively. If today's luck favours one player scandalously, tomorrow's may smile upon his opponent. We cannot possibly ban chance from backgammon.

The doubling cube confuses things in tournaments. Extra rules are required to accommodate it. The cube is ideal for individual matches, where winning money is paramount. But from tournaments it should be excluded.

This, though, is a personal opinion.

9

ETIQUETTE

The old story of the courtesan who played backgammon with the Emperor and laughed at his dice rolls (and, of course, he was beheaded) may seem a curious introduction to a chapter on etiquette or proper conduct. One is entitled to enjoy the difficulties of one's opponent. But one should never laugh in front of him!

Etiquette in backgammon, in common with most other games, is an unwritten code of practice. It is split into two sections: commonsense and formal behaviour.

Most of the code is commonsense. Everybody over twelve should know what is correct and proper, and what is naughty (or even nasty). Some players, not necessarily gamblers, depend so much on victory in a game that they may become unsportsmanlike in their efforts to secure it. There are many examples. For instance, the player who tries to distract the attention of his opponent or the one who blows smoke into his face or the one who incessantly whistles or hums tunes. The best advice to the beginner is to think of backgammon as a game that depends so much on dice that no defeat can lead to disgrace. Winning at all costs is an unmistakable sign of immaturity. Avoid being nasty to your opponents.

The second branch of etiquette deals with formalities. Most of them may sound exaggerated when you play with your wife or daughter, but they become necessary in clubs and tournaments, when backgammon is a fierce contest rather than a delightful pastime.

Not all backgammon players are faultless, and the rules are there to prevent abuse.

First and foremost, you must learn how to handle the dice properly. They are the most sensitive part of the game's equipment. You must place them in the dice cup, shake them well and throw them in your right-hand table. If a die jumps out of the table or does not fall square, then you must throw both dice again.

If the throw is correct, you should not touch the dice again before completing your moves. Your opponent must not have to rely on his memory. He should be able to see what moves you are doing. When you have finished your moves, you should pick up the dice and place them in your dice cup, ready for your next throw.

You should never take away one die as an indication that you have played that number. This is misleading. Both dice should be thrown and retrieved together.

The way you move the men is also of paramount importance. You may *not use both hands* to make the moves. This distracts the attention of your opponent and could make him suspect that you are attempting to cheat. Use one hand and move the men *one by one*, enabling your opponent to check what you are doing.

Tentative moves may become a headache. Some allow them, others refuse even to consider them as legal. But tentative moves have no place in any serious competitive game. An average player should be able *to visualise* the consequences of a move. The old French saying *toucher-jouer* ("When you touch a piece, you must play it") should apply in all board games. It keeps the game clean and allows both players to derive full enjoyment of their favourite pastime.

I suppose this is the ultimate objective of all the rules on etiquette.

10

THE TABLES' FAMILY

Backgammon is not the only game that can be played on the Tables' board. There are scores of other games, some of them out-dated, some forgotten and some just underrated.

The vast majority of the out-dated games are those which depend so much on the fall of the dice that the skill factor is limited to an unacceptably low level. They do not reach the minimum of 25% skill, which makes backgammon such a balanced game.

In *Plakoto*, for instance, the skill factor is reduced to about 5%. It is still a pleasant game in its unpredictability, but it does not offer any serious challenge. Sometimes it virtually ends after the first three or four turns. Some other games – like Dutch Backgammon, Russian Backgammon or Snake – are just curiosities or museum pieces. They would need a radical uplift to stand on their feet again. None of these games, therefore, merit a detailed description here.

Only *Moultezim* and, to a lesser degree, *Ghioul* offer the desired balance of skill and luck; both reputedly coming from Turkey. Extensive testing has shown that the skill factor in Moultezim is fractionally higher than that of backgammon. It may be as high as 35%! This makes it a game of considerable skill. If you asked me why it is almost unknown in Europe, I would answer with a cryptic clue: "because it can afford to wait!"

A real aristocrat among the Tables' games, it has been played for centuries by an exclusive circle of Sultans and Pashas who. like the medieval fans of *Arithmomachia* –

bishops and scientists – did not care to attract the masses to the delights of their exclusive enjoyment. Outside its native land, Moultezim still remains the game of the initiated few.

True, its initial phases are somehow slow. Perhaps it does not offer the instant suspense and excitement of backgammon. Yet if you would like to savour the essense of the Tables' board, it is Moultezim that you should choose as the worthy alternative to backgammon. It is so much deeper than any other dice game that it deserves the attention of the backgammon player, and it is highly recommended.

Ghioul is its twin sister. Although it is largely based on Moultezim, a change in the handling of the doubles makes it so complicated that it needs a large computer to analyse it rather than the limited human brain. Strangely enough, this difficulty makes it almost insoluble and consequently reduces the skill factor. I have a feeling that when computers eventually come to dominate the field of games, Ghioul may be proclaimed the indisputable king of the Tables' board. For the time being, however, that throne is shared between backgammon and Moultezim.

How to play Moultezim

Moultezim is played like backgammon, but with the following differences:

— All the fifteen men of each player are placed initially on the same point as in Diagram 69.

— White and black men move in the same direction – anticlockwise.

— There are no blots. Each point occupied even by a single man is closed to your opponent's men.

— To start with, you may only move one man until he gets as far as your opponent's starting table. Diagram 70 shows in which table your first man has to land, before you are entitled to move your other men at all.

— You may occupy, if you are able, all the points in a

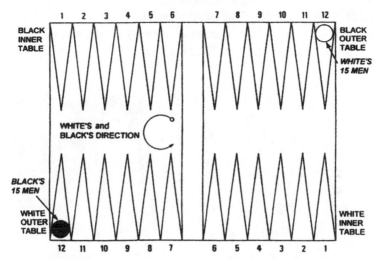

69. *Moultezim*: the initial arrangement. Note that both black's and white's pieces move in the same direction (anticlockwise), and that the inner tables are not facing each other. The system of notation has also changed.

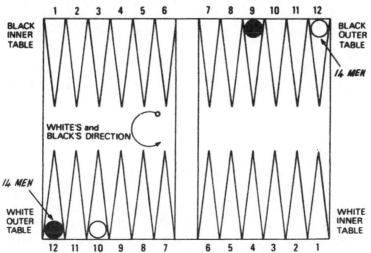

70. *Moultezim*. Both sides have reached the opponent's starting table (which is their own outer table) and they now can play their men freely.

table, *except* the starting table of your opponent (which is, incidentally, your outer table), where you may occupy a maximum of four points. Diagram 71.

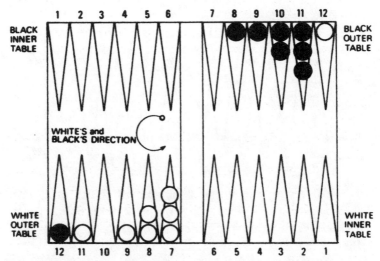

71. *Moultezim.* Throughout the game, players are not allowed to occupy *more than four points* in their opponent's starting table.

— Doubles are played in the same way as in backgammon.

Strategy

It would take a large volume to examine all the implications of Moultezim's moves. The best strategy, in brief, is to make primes – six consecutive points occupied by your men. These will prevent your opponent from moving and, at the same time, enable you to choose your plays. The most effective primes are those closest to your inner table. Primes close to your opponent's inner table may have a disadvantageous effect.

It is not advisable to advance to your inner table in the first stages of a game. Moultezim, by its nature, requires small gradual steps and large concentrations of pieces. If you manage to split your men into two large groups, almost any strategy will work for you.

Because of the high skill factor, games between players of equal strength are usually decided in the last few dice rolls.

How to play Ghioul

Ghioul is played like Moultezim with the following exceptions.

— If you are unable to play a dice throw, your opponent must play it, if he is able. *Example*: You have thrown 5–3, but you are unable to play 5. Your turn is not over by playing 3. The move passes to your opponent, who must play 5, if able. On the other hand, if you are unable to play either number, then your opponent *must* play the whole 5–3 if able. Then his own turn follows.

— A double throw is followed by *all* the remaining higher doubles. For example, after throwing 3–3, you must play 4–4, 5–5 and 6–6. If unable to play all or part of the turn, your opponent must continue from where you left off. Should your opponent also be unable to continue, the turn is over. So your opponent finishes the rest of your turn as far as he is able, and then has his own throw. In other words, the right to continue the unplayed numbers passes from you to your opponent (or vice versa), but it does not come back again.

Strategy

You must make room for possible doubles. It should be appreciated that by rolling a 1–1 you may clear up the board under the eyes of your opponent, who would be unable to do anything other than watch you playing!

Ghioul is so difficult to play scientifically that it becomes a "fun game" depending almost entirely on luck. Diagram 72 shows what it may become by throwing 1–1. The position is hypothetical.

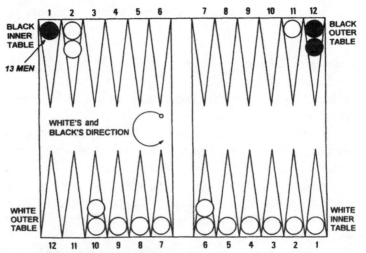

72.   *Ghioul.* Black throws 1–1 and is unable to play (white B11 blocks black's B12). In spite of having 13 men on his 1 point, black loses the game to white who, after moving all his men into the inner table, throws again 2–2!

11

EXPERIMENTS ON
THE BACKGAMMON BOARD

INTRODUCING DOMINO AND DICELESS GAMES

Although the best games of the Tables' board – like backgammon and moultezim – are complete and need no revision, one often wonders what the outcome might be if the element of luck was drastically reduced or completely eliminated.

Hitherto this was a hypothetical question for there was no such thing as a backgammon game of pure skill. In this chapter, however, I shall give the reader a choice of two diceless games:

— TILES, in which the dice are replaced by dominoes – and you may play the whole range of the conventional games.

— GRASSHOPPER, a game of pure strategy, like chess, where you move your men in accordance with a tactical plan.

However I caution the reader that the "feel" of these games is entirely different from that of the ordinary backgammon. For instance, when you need a 4–3 in backgammon, you can only pray for it. Even if you are mathematically orientated and know your probabilities chart by heart, your knowledge could not persuade the dice, I am afraid, to show a 4–3!

In the diceless variations you need not resort to prayers. By studying your position you know at a glance whether a 4–3 move is available to you, just as a chess player knows whether his rook is able to make a desired move.

What you should keep in mind when playing these variations is that the game of backgammon has undergone a shattering transformation. Of course, you still use the same equipment and strive to reach the same goals, but you should change your criteria; you should prepare yourself to adopt a game with a radically different personality. On the other hand, the satisfaction in winning will be complete, for you will know it was *your* ability and *your* superior strategy that have beaten your opponent.

TILES *(by Matt Crispin)*

General

Properly speaking *Tiles* is not a game. It is rather *a way to play games* on the Tables' board by using dominoes instead of dice. The skill factor goes up to 75–85%.

Each game is treated here on its own merits. For instance, the rules for Domino Backgammon differ from those of Domino Moultezim – and Ghioul's rules differ again. For each game there is a special "program", which has to be individually prepared. Some rules, too, have had to be modified.

Dominoes

All the games are played with a double-six set, from which you discard the seven blank tiles (4–0, 0–0, etc.). Then you split the remaining twenty-one tiles into two groups: the doubles, on the one hand, and the remaining fifteen tiles on the other. The two groups together contain all the possible dice rolls. Depending on which game you play, the doubles are subjected to special rules.

Distributing the dominoes

The first player takes eight of the fifteen tiles, plus three doubles. The second player takes the remaining seven tiles plus three doubles.

In friendly games, where the chance factor is welcome, the tiles are placed faced down on the table and thoroughly shuffled. Then the players alternate in taking one tile at a time. The doubles are in a separate pile and their distribution is pre-determined (see below).

In tournament and "intellectual duels", where the players' talent is at stake and consequently the skill factor should be paramount, the tiles are distributed in accordance with the following 'fair-share' plan.

FIRST PLAYER	SECOND PLAYER
6–6	5–5
3–3	4–4
1–1	2–2
6–4	6–5
6–2	6–3
	6–1
5–4	
5–3	5–2
5–1	
	4–3
4–2	4–1
3–1	3–2
2–1	

Note that the doubles are *always* distributed as above.

Preliminaries

The board is placed between the two contestants as in the ordinary dice game. The men are arranged in their initial position, according to the game you have chosen to play. Each player's dominoes are placed in two groups on his right, as in Diagram 73; one group consisting of the three doubles, the other of the remaining tiles. All the tiles should be *face upwards* and in the full view of both players.

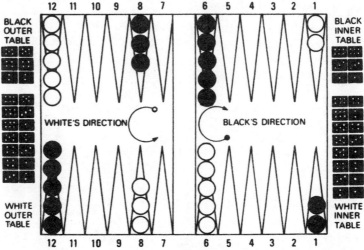

73.   Preliminaries to a DOMINO game. The initial position of the men depends on the game to be played – backgammon in this case. Note the face up dominoes, right and left. Black's dominoes are on the left, white's on the right.

The first player chooses any tile – except a double (for the doubles, special rules apply), places it in his right-hand table, and plays as if it were a dice roll. The tile is then placed *face down* on the table and is temporarily out of play.

The game alternates on these lines until all the tiles of both players have been played, with the exception of the doubles.

Then the two contestants swap their tiles (except the doubles) and continue their play. Over the course of a game, the contestants may swap dominoes three or four times. Thus each player is certain to have the opportunity to play all the available dominoes at least once (except the doubles).

Doubles

· The doubles are not interchangeable and are subjected to special rules, which vary from game to game. Extra rules apply in backgammon and different ones in Ghioul. But the basic rules are the same in all games.

— The first player takes the sixes, the threes and the ones.

— The second player takes the fives, the fours and the twos.

— You are not allowed to play a double before the first swap (change-over) of tiles.

— Doubles are *not* changed over. Unlike the other tiles, they always stay with the same player.

— They are not repeatable either. Once you have played a double it is permanently out of play for the rest of the game.

— In backgammon and moultezim they are played in arithmetical order, lower first (in Ghioul it does not matter). In backgammon, for instance, the first player must play his 1–1 first, then proceed to 3–3 and finally to 6–6.

– To play a double, you must "sacrifice" one of your other tiles. For example, you may sacrifice your 2–1 (by turning it face down, without moving your men accordingly) before playing a double. This is all one move.

Let us now examine the special rules for each game.

Domino Backgammon

You arrange the men as in regular backgammon. White always plays first.

106

In the first three moves, you are not allowed to move your "runners" – that is the two men stationed in your opponent's inner table.

From the fourth play onwards, you may move any men on the board.

Even if unable to make a move (because, for example, you have a blot on the bar that cannot re-enter) *you must* play a domino. This represents a "lost" dice roll. You simply turn it face down. But you must play a playable domino if possible, e.g. if your opponent has the fourth point vacant in his inner table and you have to re-enter a blot, you are not allowed to "lose" a move deliberately by playing (for example) a 3–5 if there is a 4 available.

For the doubles refer to general rules. Note that each contestant must play them in arithmetical order, any time after the first change-over of dominoes, and must miss ("sacrifice") one tile for the right to play each.

Strategy

As no player is allowed to move his two "runners" before the fourth move, you may try various combinations to make your bar point (7) and control at least four consecutive points around it. This – and the non-availability of the doubles throughout the first phase of the game – enables both players to build barricades, and thus keep their opponent's runners trapped. One way to make your bar point and barricade the surrounding area is shown in Diagrams 74, 75 and 76, where both players – after their third moves – have built a good defensive wall. It will be another five moves, at least, before they are allowed to play their first double!

The doubles must be used sparingly, for they are irreplaceable. They could win you the game, if you save them for the bearing off phase. You have to look ahead of the particular

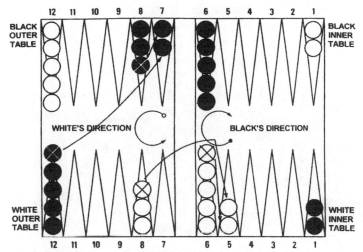

74. DOMINO BACKGAMMON First move: White 3–1. Black 6–1. Both players make the standard moves.

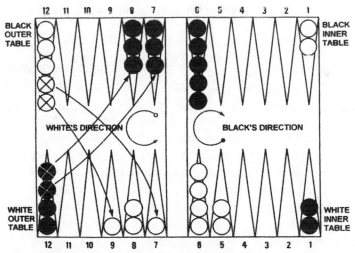

75. DOMINO BACKGAMMON Second move: White 6–4. Black 6–5. Note that the "runners" are not allowed to move before the completion of the third move.

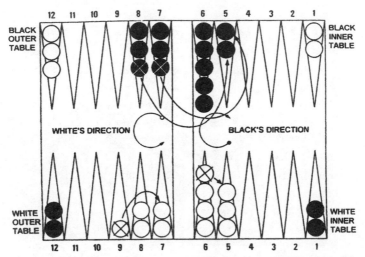

76. DOMINO BACKGAMMON Third move: White 2–1. Black 3–2. Both players have made four points to keep their opponent's runners trapped. From next (fourth) move there are no restrictions in the moves of men, except that doubles must not be played before the first "swapping" of dominoes.

requirements of a position before committing your doubles. Sometimes it is preferable to play them in the initial phases – perhaps as soon as you are allowed to.

The most important factor of domino games is that as you play, your hand goes on diminishing. What is more, your opponent knows what is left to you. So when you play your last two tiles, before changing over dominoes, you will be highly vulnerable. He will know that you lack at least two numbers and he may expose blots that he would not have dared to in a dice game. It is in this phase that the better all-round player takes advantage.

Domino Moultezim

As we have seen already, Moultezim is one of the fairest and most skilful games available on the Tables' board. With dominoes, the skill factor goes up to 90%.

The rules are the same as in domino backgammon, but as the initial position of the men and the abolition of blots make it quite different, the dominoes produce exciting situations and closely fought endgames. As there are no runners, the rules on them do not apply. But the doubles are "freed" after the first changeover of dominoes, as in backgammon and Ghioul.

For this reason it is best that, in a match, the overall number of games should be even, provided that the players take turns to start. Eight games is a good number. If one of the contestants takes five, he wins. If it is a tie (4–4) the points are taken into account, as explained next.

In every game the winner is credited with a number of points, depending on the position of his opponent's pieces. He earns for each man left to his opponent:

— *One point*, if he were in his (the loser's) inner table.

— *Two points*, if he were in any other table.

So in the case of a tie in the number of games, the player who has earned more points is the winner.

The rules on doubles are similar to backgammon.

Strategy

It follows the same lines as the dice game. You should try to make at least one prime as close to your inner table as possible.

Domino Ghioul

This is played like the dice game, with the following exceptions:

— The doubles are distributed as in other domino games, but they can be played in *any order*, after the first swap of dominoes.

— Each double must be followed by its complementary double, so that the two total 7. For example, fives must be followed by twos, and so on. Here is the complete list.

> 1–1 and 6–6
> 2–2 and 5–5
> 3–3 and 4–4
> 4–4 and 3–3
> 5–5 and 2–2
> 6–6 and 1–1

Each double must be followed by its complementary double *in the same turn*, i.e. double twos by double fives, double ones by double sixes and so on, no matter whether or not the fives and sixes have been played previously.

Strategy

Ghioul, by its nature, is an extremely difficult game in any form – dice or dominoes. The rule that when you are unable to play a dice roll wholly or partially, your opponent must play what you have left unplayed if possible, makes it unpredictable for beginners. The domino version is easier than the dice, since the number of doubles you are required to play is reduced. Nevertheless you may win your first matches by fluke rather than by superior strategy or foresight. It is still more confusing for the beginner than backgammon, but there is plenty of room for skill and entertainment.

GRASSHOPPER – THE DICELESS BACKGAMMON

Invented by Matt Crispin

In Grasshopper you do not have to think of dice and dominoes or numbers that have to be converted to moves. You have to think of it in terms of positioning your pieces, rather than simply moving them *so many* points further. From this point of view, Grasshopper may be compared to Draughts or Nine Men's Morris. It is a game of pure strategy, in which the skill factor is 100%.

What you have to do when playing Grasshopper is to concentrate on the board and forget everything about numbers and *formulae*.

General

This is a collective racing game of pure skill for two players. It is played on an ordinary backgammon board, without dice, for the element of chance has been replaced by that of rational planning.

Equipment and preliminaries

Each player has *fourteen men* of a distinctive colour. We shall follow the already established convention and call them black and white. Beginners are advised to use fewer men in their first games, but never less than eight. The number of men must always be even (i.e. 8, 10, etc.).

For easy reference, the notation has had to be revised.

As the men of both sides move in *the same clockwise direction* – in fact they start and finish in the same tables – the four tables have been given a letter, from A to D, and their points are individually numbered from 1 to 6.

Diagram 77 shows the starting and finishing tables, the direction of movement and the new notation system. Both players start in Table A and move through B and C to finish at Table D, where the bearing off takes place.

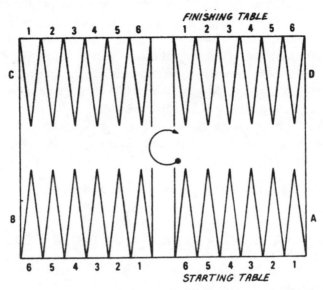

77. GRASSHOPPER Table A is the common starting point and Table D the common "finishing line". The move is clockwise for both sides. Note the notation system: each table is separately numbered.

Object

To win, a player must score twice in succession – though not necessarily in two consecutive moves. To score, a player has to manoeuvre two of his men into Table D, build a wall (see below) and bear it off. A winning score therefore is made when two walls of the same colour are borne off successively. A wall consists of two men of the same side placed on the same point. Diagram 78.

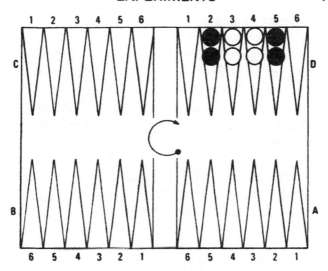

78.   GRASSHOPPER Scoring or bearing off process.

Example: if the first player bears off a wall from the last table (D) he has an advantage point against the second player. Then, if the second player bears off a wall, the advantage is transferred to him. In simple language, the player who last managed to bear off a wall has the advantage. See below *Movement and Walls*.

How to start

Use any agreed method to determine who plays first. At the outset the board is empty. The game begins with the first player introducing a piece onto any vacant point in Table A. The second player follows suit. After the introduction of the first two pieces, players have, in turn, the choice between the introduction of a new piece when there is a vacant point in Table A, or moving a piece which is already on the board.

Movements and Walls

Single pieces may move to any vacant point in the *next table*. Example: a piece in Table B is not allowed to advance to any vacant point of the same table (B), but it can advance to any vacant point of the next (C) table.

A wall consists of two pieces of the same side, one on top of the other.

To build a wall:

— The pieces must be in adjacent tables, for instance A and B or B and C or C and D.

— And they must occupy *points of the same number* (matching points), for instance B3 and C3.

Once a wall has been built no single piece *of any side* can jump it. Consequently, there might be occasions when a player is temporarily unable to move. This does not freeze play. The other player is allowed to continue his play, until the immobilised player has the opportunity of moving again.

Diagram 79 shows how to build a wall. The man on A2 can move to B2 and build a wall there. The man on B2 cannot possibly build a wall on C2, as that point is occupied by the opponent's side. Finally, the man on C2 cannot build a wall on D2, for no single man can jump a wall.

The top piece of a wall has a particular freedom denied to the single piece: it may jump as many walls as there are in its way, provided that beyond them there is either a vacant point to land or another piece of its own side on which to build a wall. In all other respects its moves are governed by the same rules as are the single pieces.

In Diagram 80, the single piece on A4 cannot move to B4 where there is a potential base, for it cannot jump the wall on B3. In fact this piece cannot move at all, for the two points before the wall (B1 and B2) are already occupied. It does not matter by whom.

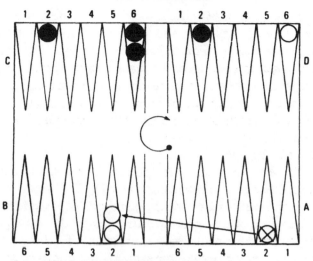

79.   GRASSHOPPER Building walls.

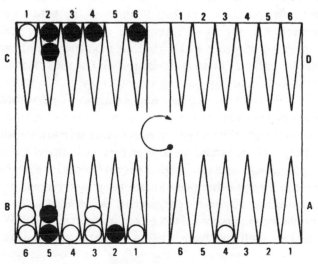

80.   GRASSHOPPER Moving through walls.

Another example on the same diagram: the top piece of the wall on B5 may jump the walls on B6 and C2 and land on the vacant point 5 on Table C.

Note that *no more than two pieces* may be placed on the same point, and both must belong to the same side.

End game

Once a piece has moved into Table D, *the finishing line*, it is immobilised there, for no further move is possible. But if another piece of the same side advances to the same point, then both pieces, as a wall, are available for bearing off. Put simply, you can take the wall off the board *in one go*, scoring one point.

The player who scored last has a chance, by scoring again, to win. On the other hand, if players alternate in bearing off walls, the result will be a tie.

Imagine that in Table D – the finishing line – there are three walls, one black and two white. If the white wall is borne off, his opponent must bear off the black wall at once, otherwise white will win in his next move by bearing off the second wall (two walls in a row). On the other hand, if black is forced, by having no other available move, to bear off his wall first, white wins against any opposition, in his next two moves.

Occasionally, the last two pieces of one side are so placed that they cannot build a wall in the finishing line. For example (Diagram 81), one piece is on C5 and the other on D3. If there is no other possible move, you must move your piece on C5 to any vacant square of Table D and then, on your next move, take it off the board without scoring. White can make a wall and bear it off in his subsequent move.

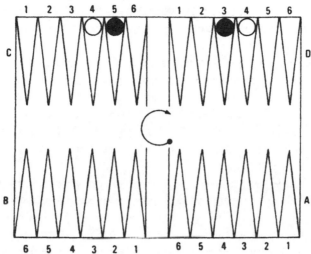

81. GRASSHOPPER Playing the last four pieces.

Advanced game

If you ever become a masterclass player and you feel that the number of draws with players of your class is too high for comfort, do not increase the number of pieces (this will simply prolong the game), just draw on a large piece of paper a five-table board, with six points on each table, in the form of a pentagon. The rules are the same except that you bear off from the fifth table.

Strategy

Grasshopper gives an equal chance to both players.

Since it is both a building and a racing game, fast, isolated pieces running to the finishing line are not effective. You should advance cautiously in small or large groups and try to build a "ladder" or "supply line". A supply line is built by occupying points of the same numbers in two or three adjacent tables. For example, A2, B2, C2 and so on.

You cannot build walls on Table A, where you introduce your pieces. But you can cut off the supply line of your opponent by occupying the point that leads to his wall. For example, if he has built a wall on B4, you must hurry to occupy the A4, thus cutting off the supply of continuous reinforcements. The player with the better supply lines should win.

Generally speaking, beginners are advised to adopt a "safe" tactical approach, advancing cautiously and building walls.

A more adventurous strategy is to land first on points where an opponent may build walls, but this can be applied successfully only with greater experience.

While beginners often achieve "lightning" victories (mostly by fluke) a game between two experienced players is usually decided by the last four and often the last two pieces. It is worth practising the deployment of pieces over the whole playing area.

POSTSCRIPT
NOTES IN THE MARGIN

Now that you know the rules and the elementary principles of "The Game of the Kings", as backgammon has been nicknamed, you should start applying your knowledge. The best way to do so is to become a member of your local club or meet friends who play backgammon. Thankfully, there are many around.

From your first contests you will realise that no matter how well you have assimilated the theory of the game – or any game, in fact – only experience and practice can help you to appreciate its finer points, and perhaps re-define the meaning of skill. "Skill" in backgammon is not the same as skill in chess. Every time you throw the dice, you face a command that cannot be avoided. Your skill is in how you adapt yourself to the commands of the dice! You cannot evade them.

Two-thirds of the game are dominated by dice rolls. It is only for the remaining one third that you are really responsible. So no defeat can be a disgrace. You have to remember this. Time and again you may think that the dice have conspired with your opponent. This is a natural feeling, for the desired roll only comes occasionally. Consequently, most players become superstitious. They fear this, they love that . . .

The human element
I shall never forget a backgammon player who somehow

had come to think that my presence at his table brought him good luck – provided, that is, that I was sitting on his right! Whenever I dared to sit on his left, he asked me unceremoniously to change over! Yet that man was a prominent doctor and an extremely good chess and bridge player. As a bridge player, he considered Hearts to be his lucky suit. "With a strong hand in Hearts," he used to say, "who cares what the others have?" Incidentally, this cost him a fortune! In chess tournaments he liked to sit down at the table second, and while he normally held his pieces with his thumb and index finger he always handled the Queen with his index and other fingers! You may wonder whether these obsessions had any adverse effect on his professional ability. As far as I am aware, the answer is an unequivocal no.

The effect of backgammon on the mood and the character depends on each individual and his particular circumstances. I knew a very successful industrialist, who also was a master chess player and prominent composer of positional studies. All his friends thought that chess was his sole obsession. Yet we found him one day, to our astonishment, happily playing backgammon! "What's the matter with you?" we asked. "Have the chess pieces disappeared from the face of the earth?" He did not answer at once – he just continued his game. Later, however, he revealed that chess problems, especially when composed or solved at night, caused him insomnia, followed by migraine the day after. "I still love positional studies . . . during the day time," he added. "At night, though, I find it more soothing to play backgammon. Ever since I took it up, I have slept better."

In any stressful situation a game may relax you and bring peace of mind.

It is true that Plato and Montaigne were somehow sceptical about games although they did not actively dislike them. Plato thought that the spirit of his ideal city might be spoiled by the "pariahs" who passed their time "dicing and moving pawns around". Montaigne was not so abosolute: he thought that games might reveal a frivolity of character, but he did not seem to condemn the players. He probably believed that so-called "scientific games" take too much time to be tackled.

Thankfully, no single philosopher, however great he may be, can change the course of history. And what history teaches us is that games have been a part of the human civilisation, an indispensable part that one cannot possibly ignore.

Coming back to our own times, when bestiality and inhumanity have reached unprecedented heights, we can find enough evidence of the power that games exercise on the mind. In THE RED ORCHESTRA, the author, who incidentally was himself indifferent to games, expresses his admiration of their power to strengthen and reinforce morale, by telling us the story of the wrongly imprisoned general, who managed to survive and keep himself sane by making chess pieces with bread and playing on the floor of his cell with the other prisoners!

Some time earlier, the Austrian writer Stefan Zweig, in a famous short novel, THE ROYAL GAME, referred to the plight of a prisoner of conscience in Hitler's Germany, who was held incommunicado and in conditions of strictly imposed silence – and yet he managed to survive and retain his sanity by playing through a book of chess games, which had been accidentally left in his cell! Although he was not a good chess player himself – he understood little more than the moves of the pieces – the games offered him a distraction from his predicament. They proved to be a better helpmate for him than anything else (even another book), for once he had learned the games by heart, he amused himself by trying different moves and sometimes improving upon the strategy of the Grand Masters . . .

And when his captors discovered the source of his fortitude (the book) it was too late for this to harm him, for the prisoner had come to know the games by heart and continued to play on an imaginary board. No-one could deprive him of his cherished possession! The most amazing twist of the novel comes at the end. When he was freed, chess reverted to the right dimensions; it became, once more, a pastime. All the same, he had become, as he realised to his astonishment, a Grand Master himself!

Creativity and style
Some people find that moving a cheap piece of plastic on a paper board is more than just a way to pass the time and divert attention from problems. They claim – and I quite agree with them – that games have got not only a negative side but also a positive one. By "negative side" they refer to the element of escapism, while by "positive side" they mean the encouragement of constructive thinking and dedication to an objective.

To this theme there are as many variations as there are players. But, generally speaking, we may divide the "creative" players into two broad categories:

Those who find a game compatible with their personality and thus can express themselves through it.

And those who try to penetrate and analyse the very structure of a game.

Both classes are creative but they express themselves in different ways. Those who find that a game agrees with their personality usually become good players. The Grand Masters in chess and in *Go* belong to this category, as do the often anonymous great backgammon and bridge players.

Within the second category belong the innovators and inventors as well as those who research the fundamental theory of a game.

The link between great players and inventors is their common love for games. Despite the fact that games rarely earn a living for those who are dedicated to them (with some notable exceptions), they all consider themselves professionals.

From their point of view, it was not laziness, or fear of the struggles in the outside world, that sent them to the games table. Games are their mission. And while they are willing to admit that their initiation may have been prompted by a need for escapism, they have come to appreciate the advantages which accrue to the players as against the non-player.

To conclude this postcript, I hope the reader does not mind if I recount a personal anecdote. During the Second World War I had to live in hiding for about two years. I was a very young man then, and that compulsory self-imprisonment was disturbing and indeed suffocating. In the next room there lived another young man in the same circumstances. Although we felt sympathy for each other's fate, we had little else in common, and all our attempts to communicate were fruitless.

One day, however, he saw a box on a shelf and asked me whether it was a backgammon board. My answer was in the affirmative. In the next twelve months, backgammon became a link – the only possible link – between us and the outside world. It was so addictive that we agreed to limit our playing sessions to the evening hours only. What is more, it was rewarding. It created an illusion of social life and contributed to our survival.

Ever since, when we meet, it is the small, miracle-working backgammon board that we most remember of that period. It gave us a sense of inner freedom, which was exactly what we most needed at that time.

INDEX

NOTES

NOTES